THE WINES OF PENTAGOËT

BOOKS BY JOHN GOULD

New England Town Meeting
Pre-Natal Care for Fathers
Farmer Takes a Wife
The House That Jacob Built
And One to Grow On
Neither Hay nor Grass
Monstrous Depravity
The Parables of Peter Partout
You Should Start Sooner
Last One In
Europe on Saturday Night
The Jonesport Raffle
Twelve Grindstones
The Shag Bag
Glass Eyes by the Bottle
This Trifling Distinction
Next Time Around
Stitch in Time

With F. Wenderoth Saunders
The Fastest Hound Dog in the State of Maine

With Lillian Ross
Maine Lingo

Novels
No Other Place
The Wines of Pentagoët

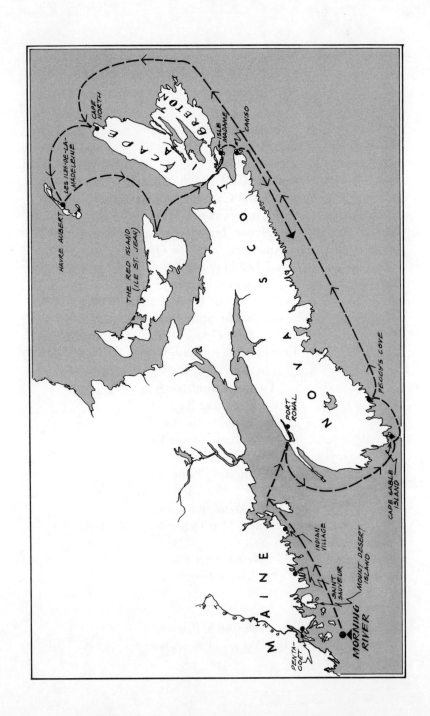

THE WINES OF
PENTAGOËT

JOHN GOULD

W · W · NORTON & COMPANY
NEW YORK   LONDON

Copyright © 1986 by John Gould
All rights reserved.
Published simultaneously in Canada by Penguin Books Canada Ltd,
2801 John Street, Markham, Ontario L3R 1B4
Printed in the United States of America.

The text of this book is composed in Janson, with
display type set in Goudy Bold. Composition and
Manufacturing by The Maple-Vail Book Manufacturing Group.

First Edition

Library of Congress Cataloging in Publication Data
Gould, John, 1908–
The wines of Pentagoët.
1. Maine—History—Colonial period, ca. 1600–1775—
Fiction. I. Title.
PS3513.0852W5 1986   813'.52   85-31991
ISBN 0-393-02303-6

W. W. Norton & Company, Inc.
500 Fifth Avenue, New York, N. Y. 10110
W. W. Norton & Company Ltd.
37 Great Russell Street, London WC1B 3NU

1 2 3 4 5 6 7 8 9 0

5015470

*Dr. Gould and Dr. Garcelon encounter a blow-down on the wilderness trail
to one of their favorite Maine trout ponds*

They's many things in this book I'm willing to accept as possible or better, but when it says Carmelle cooked gannets and they didn't taste fishy I've got to be allowed a doubt.

(Signed) Peter Partout
Peppermint Corner

Orthographic Signs

The diaeresis (French, 'tréma') shows that the vowel bearing it is divided in pronunciation from the preceding vowel, *e.g.*, Noël, naïf.
—*A French Grammar* by W. H. Fraser and J. Squair

Accordingly, Pentagoët.

This affair, insignificant enough as it was, was going to have consequences of great importance to St. Castain and would definitely influence his life.

Le Baron de Saint-Castain by Pierre Daviault

Quiconque étudie l'histoire de l'Acadie à ses débuts s'étonne que cette colonie soit si longtemps restée française malgré l'abandon de la France, à côté d'établissements anglais bien peuplés, riches, fort de milices. nombreuses, puissamment intéressés à la conquête de ce territoire.

Ibid.

The French claimed both banks of the Penobscot river, and even westward to the Kennebec, and then eastward to the Sainte-Croix. The English insisted their title included Pentagoët and beyond. We shall see that the Baron of Saint-Castain prevented the English from gaining a foothold in the area from Pentagoët to Sainte-Croix for thirty years.

History of the Abenaquis
by Abbot Maurault

THE WINES OF PENTAGOËT

1

In which the story is retold of fabled Norumbega,
and David Ingram visits the golden turrets of the
shining city of the Bashaba

There are people who take themselves too seriously and
say this David Ingram was a liar. That's what comes,
sometimes, of having an education and knowing a lot of
things that aren't so. David *was* a teller of tall tales, a
weaver of fanciful yarns—perhaps he was just our first
veracious down-Maine author—but you've got to take
into consideration what happened to him. The people
who write our history books don't always consider
everything, and their scholarly way out is just to say
that David Ingram was a liar. But, even if he was, which
he wasn't, he still deserves his rightful place in our

admiration. He was the man who brought back to England the eye-witness descriptions of the magnificent city of Bashaba, the towers of pearls and the turrets of rubies that adorned the walls of the shining capital of diamond-crusted Norumbega, where nuggets of gold were like pebbles on the beach. Not a word of truth in it, so they make the man out a plain liar. He told how he picked up two buckets of pearls, but he got tired carrying them about and hove them away. But anybody who knows anything about the State of Maine, which was Norumbega, knows that David Ingram was never really a liar. He was woods queer.

Which he had every right to be. He came from Barking, in Essex, and like a good many other English boys of his time he got caught up in sea fever. This might, and in his instance did, mean that he became a pirate, although in his day the English people favored kinder words for that profitable trade. In 1568 David Ingram was a "sailor" in the fleet of Captain John Hawkins. Hawkins was a respectable citizen who was to show talent and valor with Sir Francis Drake against the Spanish Armada, and to become the honorable treasurer of Her Majesty's Navy. Distinguished gentleman. He is less heroically described in some books as a privateer. He was a pirate, and with six vessels in his fleet he was no small fry. At the time David Ingram joined him, he was chasing down Portuguese traders laden with black captives about to be sold as slaves. Hawkins dealt severely with these unprincipled Portuguese, and then took the blacks to the Caribbean Islands where he sold them to Spanish settlers. It made a good business. Along with sideline depredations and assorted peccadilloes as they came along, Captain John Hawkins was doing all right.

But he made a small mistake somewhere, and, piqued

at him, a bunch of Spaniards set upon him in Vera Cruz harbor and just about ruined him. He escaped with two ships and about a hundred men, and put ashore on the mainland to trim ship and decide on policy. He didn't have supplies enough to bring a hundred men back to England, and a hundred men overcrowded the two ships anyway. So he just put the superfluous men ashore, wished them well, and sailed away—yo, ho, ho. One of the superfluities was our David Ingram. While David lolls on the beach down Mexico way, let us consider a couple of things:

One is the prehistoric footpath along the Atlantic coast from the Gulf of Mexico even to Labrador. It was never a trail that one took and followed end to end. Instead, it was used in the local migrations of the Amerind tribes in short stretches, as they moved place to place in their home territories. But each stretch led to another stretch, and so on, and the Long Trail was there to bring David Ingram to Norumbega.

The other thing to consider is Norumbega. The French spelled it Norumbecque. It was the word of early French explorers for the region about Maine's Penobscot Bay. It meant the river Penobscot, its course, its banks, its islands, and the open water beyond Penobscot Bay. The Indians who lived at Norumbega became the Norumbega Indians, although otherwise Penobscots, Tarratines, and Pentagoëts. A part of the Norumbega area was to become The Bagaduce to the English, from a smaller river confluent by the present town of Castine. The English Bagaduce was the French Pentagoët. At the time David Ingram was left on the beach by gallant Captain John Hawkins, Norumbega was well known to seafaring people from Europe. Ingram had heard of Norumbega. But Norumbega was by no

means explored and settled. The boats that had ventured that way—most of them—were looking, as had
Columbus, for the quick route to Cathay, and the skip-
pers hoped every river would take them right through
to Asia. But the good fishing in Norumbega Bay was
also attracting fishing vessels and David Ingram assumed
that if he could find Norumbega he could catch a ride
home. Norumbega and Bashaba. Bashaba was the Lost
Atlantis, the Mecca, the Golden Isles. So he had heard.
He had no idea how far away Bashaba might be.

It would be about two thousand miles. Indians along
the way befriended him—he was something of an odd-
ity—and set him across rivers and swamps, gave him
food, and a bow and arrows. The big hitch in this
improbable story is Norumbega—there never was any
such place. Ingram got to The Maine all right, and the
Long Trail did bring him to Bashaba. That is, the French
Pentagoët and the English Bagaduce. The original
Bashaba had been a mighty chieftain of the Tarratines
who didn't die, but walked off into the sunset to live
forever in legend. His descendants, generation by generation, became chieftains in turn and governed with
wisdom. The tribal home at The Bagaduce was thus the
city of the Bashaba. David Ingram arrived at Bashaba.
There wasn't much there. Most of the people had gone
up the river to the hunting grounds at Moosehead Lake,
and furs had been stripped from the tepees to leave bare
poles. There were no turrets of rubies and towers of
pearls. The three men still there greeted David Ingram
in French, but he knew no French. Two of the men
were young, and when Ingram arrived they were
smearing bear's grease tinctured with oil of sweetfern
on an older man who was standing naked. This was to
deter blackflies, because the three men were about to

take to a canoe and follow the other villagers upstream. The older man, it was somehow conveyed to Ingram, was the chief of the Pentagoëts, The Great Bashaba himself. Before they went upstream, however, the three Indians set Ingram over on an island, where he went aboard a French fishing vessel named *Gargarine*, Captain Rochel Champagne, and thus went to France and home to England.

Now, David Ingram began to relate his experiences. Do you blame him? Soon ministers came from The Crown to set down his words and place them on record in the archives. In the pubs, Ingram let himself go and improved everything with each telling. He told of the golden turrets of Bashaba, shining above the dark spruce trees. He told about his two buckets of pearls. About the glamorous women girded with gold and wearing amulets studded with gems. Rubies, he said, were four inches long and two inches thick, much like the diamonds and emeralds. He told of the magnificent feast offered by the Bashaba, who sat resplendent in furs and jewels, in a palace of exceeding beauty. And Norumbega became more golden, more lapis lazuli, more pearl studded and more ruby encrusted, with each mug of ale, and the tales of David Ingram stirred the stolid British to yearning. People wanted to see this Paradise, this Garden of the Hesperides, this Nirvana, this Elysium, this Isle of the Blessed—well, this Norumbega.

And it came to pass, and we should give him credit, that David Ingram told a story that led to the expansion of English interests, to the colonization of America, and in time to the Empire. We should not call a man of such importance a liar. We should not detract from his stature and blemish his name. The people who malign him need to be reprimanded. Just because there was no shining city of Bashaba, no Promised Land of Norumbega, no gold and jewels, we should pause long enough to wonder just why David Ingram said there was. He had walked the Long Trail alone. He had survived incredible wilderness hazards. Why shouldn't the bare poles at The Bagaduce look like the lofty domes of Heaven itself? David Ingram was no liar. He was woods queer. Crazy as a coot.

2

Introducing Jean Vincent de Saint-Castain, a young
man from France, whose name is now spelled
Castine; a town in Maine

The Indian village of Bashaba—Bagaduce or Pentagoët—was subject, like all Indian villages, to the occasional cleansing ceremony, but the tidy students of the
American Indians delicately avoid mention of this. There
is no reason to be coy—it was a fact of life. The resident
Indian would remove himself a certain distance into the
woods that surrounded his village, and there in the syl-
van solitude with the chatter of mudjekeewis on one
hand and the twitter of ooskijan on the other he would
relieve himself in the simple and straightforward necessity of nature's call. It thus happened that after a time

every Indian camp and village would be surrounded by
a circle of defecation which was unsanitary, unhealthy,
and unpleasant. So from time to time a chief would pro-
claim a move, and everybody would go to a new place
for a fresh start. So the Golden City of Bashaba was not
always in the same place. After weather had eroded the
cause of such removals, the people might return.

It was just about a hundred years after the visit of
David Ingram that his jewel-studded Bashaba became
anything like permanent, and that was when Jean Vincent de Saint-Castain arrived to take possession of his
domain. That would be about 1667, maybe. The old
Saint-Castain *domaine* in France could never become his,
because he had an older brother, but young Jean Vincent was of the nobility and had been brought up
accordingly. As a youngster, he had been turned over
to the Jesuits, who taught him Greek and Latin, the
sciences and philosophies, and the amenities. Since he
was of the nobility, he had been introduced at the court
of Louis Quatorze, where he handled himself well in
his proper attire, buttons and buckles agleam and his
poniard atilt. Fine-looking boy. Louis took a fancy to
him and suggested that perhaps later he might like to
come to court and go into service. But when Jean Vincent was something like fifteen he joined the Carignan
Salières, an outfit of esteem and a sort of social club for
gentlemen soldiers. The uniforms made peacocks look
bedraggled. Aside from turning out to welcome visiting
monarchs, or to march up and down to amuse the king,
the regiment had little to do except carouse and disport,
and lift a flagon to the glory of France. There was some,
but not much, likelihood the regiment would ever engage
a foe.

But Louis Quatorze found it politically expedient to send some soldiers to help the Germans, who were being bothered by the Turks. The Turks had come into Austria, had overrun Styria, and were about to cross the River Raab into Hungary and keep on going. Jean Vincent de Saint-Castain, now an ensign in the Carignan Salières, was thus by the River Raab on the last day of July, 1664, about to be attacked by the Turks. The Frenchmen had arrived in full splendor. Each soldier was in his brocaded uniform, attended by his squire and cupbearer, and by his retainers who set up his silken tent and displayed his jeweled arms. Those old wars were a lot of fun. It was great sport to hit a man on the top of his head with an ax and see how far down you could split him. The Turks could usually go all the way down through. The sight of the Frenchmen delighted the Turks and they laughed. They made fun of these delicate young noblemen with their ribbons and plumes, their powdered white perukes, and their velvet breeches and shiny dancing shoes. "Who are these maidens?"

The next morning the Turks came on, and these white-wigged maidens creamed them. It says in the book that the River Raab was clogged with the corpses of Turks. The Turks didn't stop running until they got home, but the Carignan Salières paused when the silver trumpets sounded the brandy call, and the battle and the war were over. It happened that the Iroquois Indians went on the warpath soon after that, and stirred up by the dirty English began scalping the French in New France. Louis Quatorze had an answer to that—he sent the Carignan Salières to Quebec to handle the savages. The "maidens" soon found that wilderness warfare was not much like killing Turks, but in a reasonable time the

Iroquois were subdued and here was Jean Vincent de Saint-Castain in Canada. King Louis saw no reason to put himself to further expense, and for that matter Canada needed settlers, so he disbanded the regiment and gave each soldier a farm by the St. Lawrence river—his settlement and his bonus. The Carignan Salières were thus absorbed into Canada, but young Saint-Castain was an exception.

He *was* young; his dates vary book to book, but he was still in his teens. And he ventured to ask King Louis for a special piece of land. Norumbega. He put in for the great shining city of the Bashaba, for Pentagoët. And he got it. Likely there wasn't too much red tape. Castain's father was a landed nobleman, a supporter of the king. A favor was probably routine. But young Castain also had an uncle with another kind of clout. The uncle was "the most notorious *routier* of the south." *Routier?* That's a road-runner, a highwayman, a bandit, a robber, a thief, a brigand. A Captain John Hawkins on horseback. King Louis needed all the help he could get and was favorably inclined towards this uncle. Pentagoët? Why not? The tall tales of David Ingram had long been dismissed as tall tales, and King Louis didn't look upon the city of Bashaba as a great asset. "Let the boy have it!" And because King Louis was an adroit politician, he added, "And see that the baron his father is informed."

While young Castain was waiting for his papers to come from France, he lived with the Montaignais Indians long enough to pick up some of their tongue, and to make useful friends. The Montaignais, like the Abenaquis and Tarratines down in The Maine, had not joined the Iroquois but had stayed on good terms with the

French. When Castain learned that Norumbega was his, he packed his belongings in a chest and carried it to the cabin of Father Jacques Bigot, a Jesuit who had helped him with his correspondence to France about Norumbega. The priest promised to have the chest come to Norumbega by ship, one way or another and sooner or later, and said he would ask about a chance for Castain to make the overland trip from Quebec down to Pentagoët.

That was a well-used trail, a feeder to the same Long Trail that Ingram had followed. From the seacoast at The Maine, Indians could come up either the Kennebec river or the Penobscot river, cross the height of land to Lac Mégantic, and go down the Chaudière river to the St. Lawrence. The St. Lawrence would take them downstream to seal and walrus and upstream to the Great Lakes. Castain had only to wait until a party willing to take him along should set out for the coast, and Father Bigot sent word in just a few days. It was early September when Castain started down the trail with three Indians. Stories of that trip are numerous, in both French and English. Of the Indians, two were mature, headed for Abenaquis country on the Kennebec. The third was Wenamouet, a lad of about seventeen, or about the same age as Castain. Two days up the Chaudière river the two older men were taken by skirmishing Iroquois and dragged off more dead than alive for Iroquois amusement. Castain and Wenamouet were off the trail in a swamp, trying to snare a rabbit, and escaped the attack. Wenamouet had been over the trail but once, on his coming to Quebec, but felt he could follow it and the boys pressed on. They had no canoe, and little to promise survival except Wenamouet's woods wisdom. At

Chain of Ponds, Wenamouet fashioned a raft that took them precariously and after some time to Moosehead Lake. Then blind luck caused them to find a stashed canoe with two good paddles, and from there the route to Pentagoët was all down hill.

The snowshoe rabbit of the north woods is so named because of his huge hind feet and legs, which let him scamper on deep snow. He is not a rabbit, but a hare, and he is called the "variable" hare because his fur is brown in summer and white in winter. When Castain and Wenamouet snared their first snowshoe on that trip, he was September brown. By the time they reached a Tarratine village on the lower Penobscot, it was November and the rabbits were white. Wenamouet was, of the Abenaquis, a Tarratine, so they were among friends. They got clothes and moccasins, good food and rest, and in most of the stories of that trip there is mention of how Wenamouet joshed Castain about his eyes for the young ladies who attended them while they rested. And after a few days the boys continued downstream, coming soon to Pentagoët—to the fabled city of the Bashaba—to find that Chief Madockawando had lately proclaimed a cleansing period and the place was deserted.

But Jean Vincent de Saint-Castain was home, on his own land, and he stood among the bare wigwam poles and took possession. It was just before Christmas, give or take, Anno Domini 1667. Castain had been born in France, under the Pyrenees, in 1652, third child of the Baron and Baroness de Saint-Castain. His brother was two years older, his sister one. His mother died of "the pest" that next year. His brother succeeded to the baronetcy and was soon forgotten. (The highwayman uncle enjoyed a lingering fame, but not because of his family.)

Jean Vincent, so far from home, was to become a baron in his own right, created by Louis Quatorze in 1674, because of his services to the king and to France at Pentagoët.

3

A recapitulation of the situation at Morning River
Farm, and about the lovely (and rich) Elzada, her
ugly Mavryck, and others, including the late
Jules Marcoux

When James Mavryck, one-time royal commissioner of
the Province of New York, gave Elzada Knight a wedding present of Mediterranean-blue, priceless, Salerno-
fired chinaware, any curious bystander—had there been
one—might have asked a few questions. What, for
instance, was Elzada, a forty-year-old unmarried maiden,
supposed to do with twenty-four place settings of Salerno china halfway down the coast of "The Maine,"
miles beyond any settlement Boston knew about? And,
how-come this Mavryck, the uglist man in North

America, happened to have on hand, in Boston, a white oak cask in which reposed twenty-four place settings of priceless Salerno china? Why would Elzada want that many dishes? True, Mavryck had reason to believe Spinster Elzada would shortly "nuptial" with Captain Alonzo Plaice of the coastal schooner *Madrigal*, aboard which the cask of china and the beautiful Elzada were to sail for Morning River Farm, a half a day beyond Monhegan Island and well beyond the struggling outposts of Puritan Boston. There was one question, though, that nobody on the Boston waterfront would ask. Boston was a worldly place, and there would be no curiosity as to why this cask of beautiful china was stowed on deck instead of in the hold. Cap'n 'Lon and his *Madrigal* had long been in the coastal traffic, moving from Labrador to the Windward Islands and back, in and out of every gunkhole and guzzle between. There are tricks to every trade. So Cap'n 'Lon rolled the barrel against the rail and told the port collector it was an empty cask intended for a mailbox. Being for a mailbox it had no special value and no tax was imposed. Anybody on the Boston waterfront in those days would shudder perceptibly at the thought of paying duty on fine Salerno china. Except that Cap'n 'Lon didn't say mailbox. The customs collector wouldn't have known what a mailbox was, since there was no established postal service "down east" in 1663. So Cap'n 'Lon said the barrel was to be a packetbutt. A packet was a letter or a bundle of letters and a cask was a butt. For the next half century that white oak cask, minus the dishes, was to be a packetbutt off Outer Razor Island, offshore from Morning River, just inside the ledges where a boat could come in from the open sea and approach it in quiet water. The cask had a weathertight cover and sat on a spruce piling that was moored by a chain. It went up and down with the tide, so a hand could lean over the rail of a boat and feel inside. It was big for a mailbox, but its size and a coat of red paint made it visible to passing vessels, and in those days no vessel neglected a packetbutt. After Elzada came home on that trip, with the wedding to Cap'n 'Lon a settled matter, Norman Kincaid came with his wife, Nora, and two boys to live at Morning River and manage the farm for Elzada. Norman and Cap'n 'Lon had put the packetbutt in place, and it immediately became a link with her business in Boston.

From a childless and intestate uncle she'd never set eyes on, John Townes of Salem and Boston, she had inherited a shipping business that easily made her the wealthiest woman at The Maine, an unnecessary embellishment since her father had left her well-to-do in her possession of Morning River quadrangle. Morning River Farm was not exactly a minor property. Norman Kincaid, recruited by the ugly-faced James Mavryck, found Morning River Farm an expanse of meadowland, woodland, and shoreline with tillage, gristmill, sawmill, boat shop, smithy, wharf and haulage, and two big houses with barns and sheds. Elzada and Cap'n 'Lon lived in the big house her father had built by the upper cascade of Morning River, and Norman and family had the lovely home of Jules and Marie-Paule Marcoux below. In an improbable relationship that came about by chance, Elzada's father and Jules Marcoux had teamed up back in the beginnings, and in a region long hot in dispute between France and England had continued a happy two-language companionship. Marie-Paule had been midwife at Elzada's birth, and it was no wonder that Elzada grew up equally competent in two languages. Marie-Paule had been out of Prov-

ence, and out of Provence were the *chansons pour endor-
mir* that lulled Baby Elzada in the *berceau* that Jules made
for her. Of late, since Jules and Marie-Paule were gone,
there was no traffic towards the east, where things were
French, and what did come and go by way of the packetbutt had to do with Boston and her business—Townes
Estate.

Elzada knew nothing about the business she had
inherited from Uncle John Townes, and in her happiness at Morning River didn't care to know. At first her
Boston and Salem affairs had been handled for her by
two lawyers, Blake and Smart, who had drawn her
agreement with Norman Kincaid. But afterwards this
James Mavryck, disillusioned about his job with the Duke
of York, heard opportunity thump on his door in thun-
derous cadence, and he pretty much appointed himself
general manager of Townes Estate and left Blake and
Smart with little to do but count money and speak up
if spoken to. They had no cause to murmur or repine.
Mavryck was a man of tremendous ability, a firm believer
in the future of North America, a sly contriver if occasion required, mysterious and devious, but a bilingual
gentleman of culture and decorum, and a dedicated servant of Madame Elzada Plaice. The saying was that
nobody would want him for an enemy. And come to
think of it, nobody ever did know how-come he had a
cask of crockery in Boston. Cap'n 'Lon heard he picked
it up in Haiti, which suggested connivance. Whatever
came to Elzada by way of the packetbutt from Mavryck, she signed without question, trusting Mavryck to
the hilt. Elzada never knew what she was worth, and
she never asked Mavryck, who could have told her
because he was the only person who knew. Sometimes
oftener, but once a year in April anyway, Mavryck would

appear at Morning River aboard the chandlery ketch of Townes Estate, bringing his own good cheer and all manner of goodies for everybody. The April visits were for the annual breakfast and spirit reconditioning that went with brook trout and fiddlehead ferns. He would stay at least a week, consume gallons of flip, sit with Norman and 'Lon in the boat shop, and seldom mention business at Boston. He liked to talk French with Elzada, being as competent as she was, just to tease Cap'n 'Lon, but he'd stop as soon as he got Cap'n 'Lon to say, "Aw, come on . . ."

Morning River Farm was just about halfway. It was east of the last English village at Pemaquid, and east of the island outpost of Monhegan. Eastward of Morning River would be only French, and not much of that now until Port Royal, across the Bay of Fundy. Since the days of Jules and Marie-Paule Morning Farm had no reason to think in that direction, so it was a big surprise when Norman reached into the packetbutt one day and found a packet that did not come from Mavryck at Boston. It was waterproofed with wax, tightly bound with Grand Bank ganging, and embossed with a signet. Norman reached around to pass the packet to Cap'n 'Lon, on the sternsheets, and before he got his oars in the tholepins Cap'n 'Lon said, "My gawd, Norm—the joker's been dead for years!" He showed Norman the address on the packet:

A m*sieur* Jules Poclain Marcoux
Proprietaire domaine rivière de bonmatin
L'Acadie ouest norumbecque
Nouvelle France
Urgent, affaire du roy

Norman studied the letters and said, "I make out proprietor and urgent—and Jules Marcoux."

Cap'n 'Lon said, "I never knew Jules had a middle
name. Well, this is duck soup for 'Zadie."

It was duck soup for Elzada, but before she opened
the parcel she walked with it to a window and stood for
a moment looking off over the ocean. She made no apol-
ogy when a tear ran down and dropped to the floor.
Jules Marcoux! Her second Daddy, her guide, her companion, her friend in all her growing up! She had helped
wind him in sailcloth when he died, and at his graveside
up by the pool she had repeated the catechism for his
burial service. Somebody off there in his Acadia didn't
know that Jules was gone. *Urgent, affaire du roy.* What
would the King of France know about Jules Marcoux,
and what would he want with him? Through her tears,
she read the address again, and smiled at *rivière de bonmatin.* Morning River! She broke the seal; cut the heavy
fishing cord; opened the packet. First. There were packets
that day from Boston, too, but Mavryck could wait.
Urgent business with His Majesty?

4

Bringing another letter in French from the east'ard;
Father Hermadore appears and speaks about Manny
the Portygee

The Tarratine Indians—Poet Longfellow rhymed them
with queen and scene—had in their storied Norumbega
the best situation in a thousand miles of coastline. Great
Penobscot Bay and its islands gave them ample tidewa-
ter with boundless fish. Upcountry, the Penobscot river
divided and divided again to take them to hunting
grounds for food and furs. The Tarratines were more
advanced than other families of the Abenaquis, and did
have a written language—they could communicate by
pictures. Some of their villages had permanent sod
homes; they grew gardens. Long before America was

"discovered" they had been visited by Europeans cruis-
ing their waters to explore and fish. They were visited
by Samuel de Champlain, the explorer and first governor of Canada, and thus exposed to trade. But Champlain found them already wearing clothes of European
cut, for both modesty and warmth. When the English
Captain Argal (another pirate!) "liberated" Acadia in 1613
by driving out all the French, the Tarratines continued
their friendly relationships with France by way of their
wilderness route to Quebec. But when the Pilgrims from
Plymouth came to The Bagaduce in 1626 to set up a
trading post the Tarratines welcomed them and did
business. The Pilgrim venture didn't last long. But in
those times Jabez Knight and Jules Marcoux were already
well established and secure at Morning River, "just
around the corner" from The Bagaduce—even though
neither French nor English settlers had ventured up the
estuary to find them. Neither did Jabez and Jules venture into Penobscot Bay to know much about The
Bagaduce and Pentagoët, although they heard things from
the crews of passing vessels—both French and English.
Elzada ran some of this over in her mind before she
opened the packet for Jules, urgent on the king's business. There were no possibilities she could think of that
would make the king aware of Jules. The only chance,
she decided, would have been the time Jules went to
Port Royal to get his spurious deed to Morning River
Farm from Commandant Claude de la Tour. But Jump-
ing Judas! That was long ago. Elzada read the letter and
turned to translate it to 'Lon and Norman:

> An enterprise of importance to the furthering of
> His Most Christian Majesty's colonization of New
> France will soon bring agents to your domain, to

whom you will please render whatever assistance may be requested and which you can supply.

Elzada read through the French again, to satisfy herself she had made a good translation, and then she said, "It's signed by Grandfontaine—who's Grandfontaine?"

"Nobody I know offhand," said 'Lon.

"He's at Port Royal," Elzada added.

"Not when I was there, he warn't. Last time I was there the place was seedy. Had a priest who kept six housekeepers, maybe forty half-starved dogs, and two Indians making a canoe on top the church steps. Priest looked awful tired. He bought a keg of red wine and paid with Dutch money. I never went back."

Elzada winked at Norman. "My Captain is opinionated, and knows better than that. Port Royal is quite a place. Jules used to go there when I was a little girl— he'd sail the sloop down and come back with all kinds of things. His big trip was when the French warship came here and he thought we might be better off with a French deed. He came back with one, and another thing he had was a fake birth certificate that proves my father was born in France. But Jules wasn't in Port Royal in thirty-five-forty years."

Now Cap'n 'Lon winked at Norman. "Always felt sorry for that little overworked priest!"

The mystery about the impending visit of the king's agents remained a mystery for some time. Wondering added a fillip to going to the packetbutt. Norman and 'Lon would come back and Elzada would ask, "Anything?" She meant anything further about that letter to Jules. 'Lon always said, "When there is, you'll be the first to know—Norm and I can't read that stuff."

Nothing did come, and then after many months when

something did come, it wasn't the answer. Here, again, was the waterproofed packet tied with fishing cord, but this time it didn't have the signets. And, it wasn't addressed to Jules Marcoux. It was addressed to Mme Elzada Plaice, Morning River. And on the packet was the name of the sender. Cap'n 'Lon pointed so Elzada could see, and they both broke into laughter. The sender:

HERMADORE, SJ

Father Hermadore!

When Elzada returned to Morning River after that trip to Boston, and bedded for the first time that blissful night with Cap'n 'Lon, there had been no ceremony, church or state, to legalize the union. Considering the time, place, and circumstances, there was no way to wait on the formalities. It was Manny the Portygee, who lived on Outer Razor Island and conspired with 'Lon in various undertakings, who arranged to have Father Hermadore come, after many months, to celebrate a nuptial mass in the Morning River kitchen, thus making an honest woman of the mistress of Morning River Farm. Since then, Manny had disappeared. Nobody knew what happened. Storm, iceberg—might be. Manny had flakes for curing fish on the island and fished the Bank, but otherwise traded as Cap'n 'Lon traded along the coast from Newfoundland to the Caribbean. He and Cap'n 'Lon connived on occasion in the movement of goods some might think contraband, and if trusting somebody makes for friendship, they were the best of friends. And long before the nuptials of 'Lon and Elzada, Manny had enlisted Father Hermadore as assistant in his trading. Father Hermadore had come to America as spiritual strength for a French fisheries station in Newfoundland. The Governor of the Society of Jesus at Rome felt that because Father Hermadore had taken the sacred vows of the order he should not have joined Manny in such endeavors, so to avoid any kind of contretemps between himself and the governor, Father Hermadore had simply moved from Newfoundland to Havre Aubert in *les Iles de la Madeleine*, where he could pursue his devotions in his own way whether the governor liked that or not, and where he could continue his arrangements with Manny the Portygee on the same basis. Father Hermadore never knew if he had been excommunicated, but suspected he had. When Manny brought Father Hermadore from the Magdalens to Morning River, he immediately endorsed flip as a substitute for sacramental beverages, and then performed a rousing wedding ceremony which, as he pronounced it in French, the bride rendered into English. And now, after many years, Cap'n 'Lon slit the twine on the packet with his sheath knife.

Elzada didn't translate. She just said, "He's coming!" She read through to the end and added, "Doesn't say when. Depends on a boat. Few weeks. Hopes we're well. He's fine."

Cap'n 'Lon said, "What's he say about this Grandfontaine?"

"Nothing. Doesn't mention him."

"Funny."

"Maybe not—maybe there's no connection."

"All at once we get two letters this way and there's no connection? Seems to me there's got to be."

"Does seem so."

Cap'n 'Lon said, "Be fun to see the old fart again."

It was three weeks to the day that Norman looked up to see a two-masted boat coming up the Morning River estuary, easing in with the tide and a light air. He ran to catch a line, and there was Father Hermadore in full cathedral garb, braced against the small bump when the vessel touched the wharf, and holding a huge ivory crucifix as if to fend off disaster. "Pax vobiscum!" he said to Norman and Norman shook his head. "Not me," he said. "I don't know a word of French!"

For all the clerical grandeur of Father Hermadore's appearance, he got only hearty Anglican handshakes, the good-to-see-you-agains, and the stowing of his chest in his room. And later, with flips, the conversation came to Grandfontaine, and it turned out Father Hermadore's visit had nothing to do with Grandfontaine. Fact was, Father Hermadore didn't think too highly of Grandfontaine, and even at that Cap'n 'Lon suspected Elzada was putting a better tone to his words than his French warranted. Grandfontaine had lately been appointed commandant of Acadia by the powers in Quebec, and took himself most seriously in a position that wasn't all that serious. So that was out of the way, and they sat in the kitchen, with Elzada interpreting, and relived the wedding, even to how Manny the Portygee couldn't sign the wedding certificate as a witness because he didn't know how to write his name. Cap'n 'Lon said, "Poor old Manny—I do miss him."

"Yes," said Elzada to Father Hermadore, "we do miss Manny. What do you suppose ever happened to him?"

Father Hermadore burped, looked into his flip mug, and said, "My first flip since I was here before."

While Elzada filled his mug, Cap'n 'Lon said, "Teach him to count—he's had three."

Father Hermadore returned to the subject. "What did happen to Manny?"

"We never knew."

"Never knew what? He was in good health last month."

So Manny the Portygee hadn't been lost at sea after all. He had, instead, gone back to his native Portugal on a sudden impulse to throw his fortune (which was considerable) to the House of Braganza and pave the way for Portuguese independence from Spain. In this way Manny had come into possession of his family property, rich lands along the Douro river and town houses in Oporto. Vineyards. Father Hermadore knew a little Portuguese but not very much about Portugal. He assured Elzada that Manny was very much alive, that he was now Manuel something or other de la something else, a landed gentleman with a title, and at the moment was in England on business. It was one of Manny's vessels that had brought Father Hermadore to Morning River. She had seal furs and considerable walrus ivory, and some other things, to dispose of before she would return and take Father Hermadore to Boston. Very trustworthy crew, all from the Madeleines. Oh, yes—Manny was in good shape.

"That's great," said Cap'n 'Lon. "Hope to see him again some day."

"You will," said Elzada. "Father Hermadore says he's coming this way before long." She rehashed the father's story about Manny. Portugal, emerging from Spanish authority, needed a great many imports that England was ready to supply. But Portugal had little to barter, and Manny was just the one to see how this might prove interesting. He was able to move freight in and out of England by way of Boston, drawing from his many years of coasting and numerous connections he had. Father Hermadore was most helpful. Then, Manny got into the wine business. For a long time Bordeaux claret had been the great wine of England, going back to the days of Henry II when Bordeaux was a dominion of England. About the only wine the English knew much about. But Manny worked off a shipload of port wine from his own vineyards, saving a good deal on taxes by routing it through Boston, and now port wine was being well received in England—as well as in Boston. Manny, Father Hermadore made it plain, is one of those people who never make a mistake. What was good for Portugal was good for Manny—and Father Hermadore. Yes, Manny planned to visit The Maine soon.

"Be some old good to see him," said 'Lon. "Ask him if Manny has changed much."

Father Hermadore laughed. "Manuel? Non. Toujours pareil."

Father Hermadore explained that with Portugal, business went with the Cross, and that having a priest to speak the right good words here and there had made Manny more than grateful. Elzada smiled at the cautious words Father Hermadore used to talk around his severed Jesuit membership, but when she translated no flavor of this came to 'Lon and Norman. On the other hand, Father Hermadore continued, wearing a collar and carrying a rosary had no particular value when dealing with the people in Boston. In Boston, he played the Huguenot if need be, but the man he was about to see on this trip, about port wine, seemed to have no respect either way. Curious man, said Father Hermadore. A Frenchman, but not like any Frenchman Father Hermadore had ever known. When his vessel came back for him, he would go to Boston to see this man. He was not looking forward, but the meeting was important to

Manny. A M. LaManche, he said. LaManche—probably not his right name. Strange man, this LaManche—*laid*.

Elzada started, and looked at 'Lon. "This man in Boston," she said, "is not what you'd call good looking!"

'Lon said, "It's got to be Mavryck!"

5

The remote and half-way location of Morning River Farm
spared it from all the French-English-Indian foolishness
of the 1600s. There was no road to Morning River, and
from the open ocean the spot would not be seen because
of the Razor islands. That part of the Long Trail that
once passed that way hadn't been used in a lifetime.
Vessels moving up and down the coast had no reason
to be unfriendly, and over the years many boats came
to the Morning River boat shop for repairs. The first
time Cap'n Alonzo Plaice had visited was to get a bow-
sprit replaced. There was one year the English looked
in and might have made trouble for a Frenchman, but

Elzada's father, Jabez Knight, had done the talking. Then, when a French warship came and might have made trouble for an Englishman, Jules Marcoux did the honors. There was, off and on, some French traffic in and out of Pentagoët, but Morning River wasn't involved and the folks there didn't know about it.

Over the years, Morning River had no emergencies. One time, long ago, Jules Marcoux had fouled his hand with a fishhook, and the incident was remembered as the only real "accident." He and Jabez were off Outer Razor after a barrel of cod, and except for the pain to Jules the worst part was the exertion Jabez went through to row the big dory home alone. When they cut the mitten away and got the hook out, Jules soaked his hand in rum and said he was all right. But infection set in, and it took considerable rum to bring about a complete recovery. That taught everybody to be perpetually careful.

Food was never a problem. The rich meadowland, circled by Morning River, thawed early in the spring and in the fall the water tempered the nights against premature frost. Even in driest summers, the meadow soil was moist to the crops. Jabez Knight had not been a farmer at heart, but Jules Marcoux was. And now, Norman Kincaid loved his crops and livestock, and often left important boat-shop work for stormy days and winter weather. Game was everywhere. Jules had taught everybody, including Elzada, to snare rabbits in the swamp above the upper falls, and he made traps for grouse, doves, and woodcock. Deer ranged the beech and maple ridges, yarded in winter at the swamp, and venison that wasn't used fresh went through the smokehouse for future reference. The sea, broad to the east, gave up whatever was wanted—cod, haddock, cusk,

pollock. To be used fresh, salted, and smoked. There
was an oyster bed between the Razor islands. Clams.
Lobsters. Smelts to the surfeit every spring right under
the water wheel by the mill. And sea birds. Jules Marcoux used to fit a kernel of corn on a small fishhook,
arrange a dozen or so such hooks in the mud down the
estuary, and wait for a coming tide and a flock of geese.
The geese would find the corn and Jules would pull
them in. There was never another commotion to equal
that of a goose coming in hand over hand to meet des-
tiny. Now in the air, now under water, making great
to-do, each bird submitted at last and Jules, a soft-hearted
man, liked to explain that this didn't hurt a goose one
bit. The hook, he explained, engaged in the horny bill
of the bird, touched no flesh, drew no blood, and was
painless. Elzada would ask him, if this were so, why
the geese appeared to be so unhappy. Ducks were taken
the same way, with great saving on gunpowder. Then,
on the back ridges, stood the sugar-sweet maple grove—
although in recent years Elzada's ships handled West
Indies white sugar and Morning River didn't rely on the
maples so much.

In the early days Jules used to walk to the east'ard to
acquire livestock, and now Norman made the same
errands to the west'ard. Milking cows, working cattle,
sheep, pigs, poultry, and lately a team of horses. The
birds and beasts would arrive by boat. So there was no
lack of milk, eggs, meat, and wool. Marie-Paule had
been adept at spinning, weaving, and needlework, and
now Elzada and Nora did that work. And work it was,
leaving little time for "pleasuring," but why would one
who lives at Morning River Farm need vacations? Well,
now and then Cap'n 'Lon would get sea fever and go off
for a day-sail in his sloop—feigning he was trying out a

new sail, or perhaps looking for surf clams. Morning River Farm was the nighest thing fabled Norumbega ever had to the Golden City of the Bashaba.

Some of the idyllic remoteness of Morning River diminished after Elzada inherited Townes Estate. Boston was just as far away, but there were reasons now to send an occasional message down to The Maine. James Mavryck would come now and then in the Townes Estate chandlery boat, sometimes on business and sometimes to get away from business. And after the packetbutt was put in place he set up a sort of mail service, so all passing boats checked out the butt. It was possible to get a packet to Boston in two-three days, and sometimes an answer back within the week. And as far as necessity went, either 'Lon or Norman could get a sloop under way on short notice. In winter Norman kept his sloop on mooring in open water just in case.

The two Kincaid boys were in their teens, and getting their daily schoolwork from Elzada. She never tried to bring them along in French, but she drilled them in English grammar and supposed they were as well off as boys in real schools. There had never been, from Marie-Paule's earliest days, a boat to pause at Morning River without its box of books. The library that Jabez had shelved off in Elzada's girlhood had long since expanded up the walls of the stairway and into an upstairs room. Cap'n 'Lon, who had been a stranger to books in his seafaring days, now spent a good part of his time reading, and liked to come out with occasional erudite observations—such as that Archimedes merely put into words what every deckhand already knew.

Cap'n 'Lon, who had wondered if he could stand retirement on a farm, had found that he could. He appreciated Elzada all the way—a lovely female, an intelligent woman well learned, a willing wife and understanding companion, and it was not important to him or her that she was rich. 'Lon had signed off anyway, in a pre-nuptial agreement, to make things secure for Norman and Nora, so he partook of Elzada's wealth only as a guest. But he did have on his own, tucked away in the barn, a salt-crusted sea chest that was too much for a couple of men to lift for the coins in it. He "played" with Norman's steers at first, and then found he enjoyed doing work with them. He tried to help Norman in the boat shop, but Norman was a perfectionist and 'Lon wasn't—not with woodwork. He whittled some to pass the time, and that brought on sea fever often as not. He came across the tools Jules Marcoux had used for making barrels—planes with curved blades and curious groovers. Norman was unable to show him how to use these, as Norman didn't know—Norman said coopering "was a trade all by itself." The next time Jim Mavryck came, something was said about the barrel tools, and Mavryck responded as usual.

A couple of weeks later the Townes Estate ketch arrived to put off a little man who introduced himself as a cooper, come to teach how to make barrels. He was English, newly arrived in Boston to look for work, so Mavryck put him on the Townes payroll and sent him to The Maine. He had brought a whole new set of barrel tools, most of them duplicates of those left by Jules. The man stayed three months, and when he left 'Lon and Norman were competent coopers. It didn't take him three full months to teach his trade—he stayed on a while to learn a few boatbuilding tricks from Norman. After that, Cap'n 'Lon didn't whittle much, but made a lot of buckets that got stacked across one end of the boat shop.

The Wednesday night schedule at Morning River

Farm was now well established. Elzada had proposed it when Norman first came, and it quickly became a tradition. Every Wednesday Cap'n 'Lon would go down to the Marcoux house to take supper with Nora and the boys. Norman would come up to the big house to eat with Elzada. This gave Elzada and Norman privacy to discuss the management of Morning River Farm, and after supper the others would come to join them and they'd have a family evening. Sometimes there wouldn't be all that much farm business to talk about, but Norman and Elzada had the time together anyway and the Wednesday routine was respected as immutable. Even when Mavryck was there, perhaps with impending Townes Estate business of great moment, he was excluded and he had to accept his reduced status. But when he was there, the family evenings were always that much better. The two Kincaid boys doted on him and hung on his every word. On Wednesday nights, Mavryck was no more than "the bucket inspector from Boston."

6

Father Hermadore confesses, sort of, and offers
certain philosophies worth notice; explaining
considerable

"You should have taught the boys their French," said
Father Hermadore, meaning the two fine sons of Norman and Nora. Norman was already at work in the boat
shop and 'Lon had gone to join him. Nora and the two
boys were down at the other house. Elzada and Father
Hermadore were lingering at the breakfast table in the
big house. Father Hermadore, in cassock and skirt,
shifted his weight on the stool to find a new comfort,
and reached to pick a shred of smoked salmon from an
otherwise clean plate before him. He savored the shred.
"I could tell them so many things about the world, and

so many stories of the northland."

Elzada was under no illusions about Father Hermadore. His dubious affiliation with a Holy Order and the
Church on one end, and his function in the devious pur-
suits of Manny the Portygee on the other proved him a
master of cross purposes. Besides, her tenuous Anglican upbringing at Morning River didn't leave her ardent
about anything Roman. Again, the man hardly looked
like a priest even in the garb of one with, as 'Lon said,
". . . the fat hanging down off'n him in all directions."
A Friar Tuck perhaps, but a priest, no. "It might be
just as well if they don't hear some of your stories,"
Elzada said, and Father Hermadore relished her smile.

At that, he sat in silence a few minutes. He would
purse his lips now, and be about to speak then, but he
waited until his thoughts were ready. "I was born in
Dijon. I could tell the boys something about Dijon. I
remember nothing of my mother. My father was not a
wine merchant, but worked with wines, and he thought
I was to become a worker with wines like himself. But
at the Church of Saint Jean, which was not an important church in Dijon, I served at mass and became a
favorite of Father Guy Manet, who was a cousin of my
mother. He was an unhappy little man who was forever
lamenting that his lot was to be an obscure priest and
nothing more. I never knew what he aspired to, but I
came to realize he believed the Church had held him
back. I think he saw in me a chance to achieve what he
had failed to achieve. He got me into a school and made
sure from day to day that I was mastering all I could.
But I was being taught little else except love for Our
Blessed Lady, and I could see that I was being made
ready for the priesthood. But Father Manet had other
plans, and he moved me to another school, this time to

learn some law, philosophy, my Latin, and a suspicion of medicine. But his plans went for naught; my teachers prevailed and I took the vows of the Society of Jesus. I became a priest and a teacher, but not for sixteen years to come, and then I was a man."

Elzada picked up some dishes to carry them to the shelf for cleaning. "How did you get to Newfoundland?"

"The Pope. Jesuits are teachers, bound to extend the Church, and we go where we are sent. I was unlucky enough to be ready at the wrong time and was sent to extend the Church at Port des Gouttes—to make prayers for fishermen. Fishermen! They fished because they were sent there to fish and there was nothing else. Fifty men who did not want to fish and did not like to fish— all thieves from the waterfront of La Rochelle. They came to Newfoundland with a choice—the other choice was to be hanged. Not a woman among them, and none nearer than Labrador—Eskimos. Extend the Church! Down in Acadia there were Indians to convert, and some decent people to care for, but at Port des Gouttes I had no Indians. My fifty fishermen were beyond redemption. I had nothing to do but sit there and pray for my own peace with God and twiddle my thumbs!"

Father Hermadore drew his hands together across his great front and twiddled, to demonstrate his clerical duties at Newfoundland.

"You make a good confessor," he told Elzada. "I haven't confessed in years. It is good for me. The Newfoundland winters are long. Boats came, but only for fish. We got supplies. But always the same people. Now and then a new man would come off a boat to stay, and I would hope to have a soul to save, a new one to talk to, somebody to hear my mass. I was always disappointed. One time a ship came and brought eight women. That was not enough to go around, so I quickly made them all wives at one mass before the men fought over them, and I thought that if I kept patient I would one day have some baptisms to amuse me. That first night two men who hadn't gained a bride broke in and killed a husband, and then the wife killed the two men. How quickly felicity can fade, I thought—and wisely arranged for three separate funerals. If I had been a busy priest, I would have buried all three with one mass. Don't you think the boys would like to hear some of my stories?"

"Of course they would. And just as soon as I can teach them enough French, they'll be old enough."

"You jest about me no more than I do myself. I know my faults. But I was a good priest. I said mass every day, as a Jesuit must, and like a good Jesuit I made short work of it. I had nobody to hear me, so I would only pause at the altar and be off down the other side. Those women did have children and I baptized them, and then came a day for the catechism and I couldn't find my book. Worse—I had forgotten. And after too many years, I got my reward. Manny, our friend, came to Port des Gouttes."

"How did you two get along? Manny never knew any French."

"True. But in the seminary we had some Portuguese brothers, and I knew a few words. But Manny could always make himself understood wherever he was. I saw him with Eskimos and Indians, and they'd nod and understand when Manny just used his hands. Manny walked up from his boat that day and kneeled in front of my chapel. Nobody had kneeled within a mile of my chapel in ten years, so I was glad to hurry out and give him my blessing and lift him to his feet. 'Pax vobiscum!'

I said, and Manny said, '. . . et spiritu sanctu!' Then I was corrupted. I couldn't resist. But, I have never blamed myself. I blame the Pope. He should never have sent me to Port des Gouttes. In his wisdom, and with advice from God, he should have known better. I believe now that when God saw what a mistake the Pope had made about me, in His pity He sent Manny to make amends."

Elzada had returned to her seat across the table, and she said, "Father, from what you've just said, I should have lost all my good habits years ago. You were never any more apart from the world at Port des Gouttes than I've been here at Morning River. Manny the Portygee was my friend, too, and he never corrupted me. What's more, none of us here at Morning River ever had any sustaining faith, any vows to a Holy Order, any duty like yours to live up to. You said your mass every day, but there hasn't been a prayer here at Morning River since Marie-Paule Marcoux died, and that one was short and quick. What shall I give you for penance?"

"The more the vows, the weaker the flesh. I don't need penance—I've never felt I did wrong. I hope only for understanding. I was a ripened peach on the Church's bough and might have been picked at my prime for the glory of God—which is what some old saint said in a schoolbook, hoping to adorn his death—but I was left to drop and be bruised. Manny happened by and found me to his taste. Port des Gouttes was never the same after Manny came. The boats that came before wanted only fish, and cared nothing for Port des Gouttes. They would take our fish, leave us a pittance, and we would prepare more fish. Then Manny would come and he would take our sealskins, weigh our walrus tusks, barrel our salted meats, and take our train oil. Manny gave us money, too, but money is only money. He brought us new guns, bolts of good cloth, casks of noble wines, glass for windows, and dishes and pots. And he brought us things that made music. He brought me an altar cloth and a service—can you picture me saying mass with damask and silver, with a ripe Madeira wine for the Eucharist, and not a soul there in my chapel to see? But these people who didn't come to my mass would come to my post when the music sounded from Manny's fiddles and horns. The people at Port des Gouttes never wanted The Faith so much as they wanted a good tune— and window glass. The Pope never did all that well by us, but we could depend on Manny."

"So what's the big difference between Port des Gouttes and Havre Aubert in the Magdalens?"

"None, really—and yet a lot. Same kind of outpost, ocean and rocks. Fish. But sooner or later my affairs with Manny would have come to light, and I'd get called home. I didn't want to go home."

"Couldn't you just quit and stay on your own? Give up the priesthood?"

"Certainly. But I didn't want to give up the priesthood. I like the priesthood. Even at Port des Gouttes it was a good living. The spiritual poverty was one thing, but eating and drinking and keeping warm must be considered. No matter how depraved a parish may be— and mine was depraved—basic Christian training preserves the priest's tithe and tenure. No, I was never abused, and realized that at its worst a life in the Church has its securities. There isn't a crucifix in Christendom more beautiful, or more valuable, than this one." He held out his huge ivory cross, with the Savior in agony. The delicate carving, Eskimo, would excite envy in Rome.

Elzada asked if he found more piety at his parish at Havre Aubert.

"I don't have a parish at Havre Aubert. Not one that is constituted and recognized. When I came there, Manny saw that I was comfortable. He brought timbers for my cabin, my trading post, my chapel. Even a bell. You should hear it when I step out and pull the rope! A ringing to make the bells of Saint Bénigne envious! I am the only Jesuit in the world who owns his own church. I make no reports to superiors. The Pope doesn't even know where I am. I deal only with Manny. When I first came to Havre Aubert there was no church, but since then more people have come, and I think they would get a parish if they asked for one. But why would they ask? They think my chapel is a church, and I encourage that. They could never have a better curé. I never bleed them for money—why should I? I have more than they do, and I have no bishop clamoring for his share. I marry them, I console them, I shrieve them, I bury them. I say mass if they care to come. They are good Christians, such as Christians are, and would be no better if their priest were better. When I left them to come here they gave a candle for my return, and I will have a reception when I get back. I'm spurious, I pretend, and I am loved. Meantime my warehouse is full for Manny's boats, and my people are happy that we live so well on our rocky islands at the cost of a few seals and walrus. Except for fish, only Manny's boats—nobody else tries to trade at Havre Aubert."

"I'm pretty sure from what he's said that my Cap'n 'Lon has traded at Havre Aubert."

Father Hermadore didn't smile, he laughed. "But of course! But only when Manny was there, too. When I came here for your wedding, I wasn't sure, but your captain did look familiar to me. But he never came ashore, He and Manny dealt together aboard ship, and I'd seen him but never met him. I felt it might be indiscreet to recognize him."

Father Hermadore rearranged himself so when he began to stand there might be some likelihood that his great weight would respond. After this rearrangement he rested a minute, and then stood up. He said, "I shall walk to the boat shop and back in exercise and meditation, and then will rest in the library. I feel the need to read—before dinner.'"

Elzada said, "Yes—before dinner." She watched him go along the path and wondered if it could possibly be true that the ugly man he was going to see in Boston was James Mavryck. If those two were cooking up a deal, she'd hesitate to bet on the winner. Odds to Mavryck, probably. Then she thought, "Mavryck! My God! Mavryck is *me!* What's going on?"

7

Now Father Hermadore goes to Boston, and leaves
just before Governor Grandfontaine arrives at
Morning River

Father Hermadore's daily program at Morning River
was divided equally between the kitchen table three times
a day and the library—with short constitutionals and
meditations between. He inspected the progress of
Norman and 'Lon as they worked in the shop—but
briefly and then he would be back at the books. Elzada
suggested this and that for him to read, and to reread,
and he was content. Elzada said to 'Lon, "The man is
starved for books." 'Lon said, "He more'n makes up for
it at the trough."

Father Hermadore had looked at the letter from

Grandfontaine to Jules Marcoux. He couldn't imagine what the "business of the king" might be, but he knew a lot about Grandfontaine. Grandfontaine, he said, was a pompous ass, and the less anybody had to do with him the better. Nobody liked him at Port Royal, where he swelled around in great self-importance, botching everything, and playing the part of the royal governor so everybody was obliged to bow and scrape. Never was a governor. Elzada asked, "How do you know so much about him, being off as you are?"

"He sent word he was including our Madeleines in his new Acadia, so I asked some questions about him and got some answers. There are ways. The story was that King Louis is making a big palace for himself and this Grandfontaine had something to do with the work. Good job, and something he was able to do. But then he made a pass at the Marquise de Montespan, and that was a very foolish thing for him to do."

Father Hermadore explained delicately to Elzada that the beautiful Marquise de Montespan was bedfellow for Louis Quatorze and was a no-no for this bounder Grandfontaine. Father Hermadore couldn't say, and wouldn't if he could, if Grandfontaine had prevailed and the lovely marquise had responded to his overtures, but the upshot was the lady reflected and decided her security was more important than he was. Accordingly, she whispered to His Majesty one night that there was talk throughout the court about several of the gentlemen entrusted with the construction of Versailles. She had to remain vague, of course, for want of more than rumor, but from what she had heard . . . thus and so. She named several gentlemen, none of whom had been the subject of any such gossip, and Grandfontaine was soon on a vessel bound for Quebec. He understood he had been promoted to a new and better position, a mission of extreme importance to his king and to France. Madame Montespan relaxed.

In the diplomatic pouch aboard the same vessel that brought Grandfontaine to Quebec, a letter sealed with the king's ring would ask the governor of Quebec to find something for Grandfontaine to do, and to detain him. The governor of Quebec thought a moment, and remembered that there was an opening at Port Royal. Not much going on there, but for a royal retainer who had just been kicked upstairs Port Royal was as good a place as any to be detained. The governor of Quebec charged Grandfontaine with the duty of restoring Port Royal, and all of Acadia, to something of its former importance. Grandfontaine, Father Hermadore emphasized, had never been more than a "commandant" at Port Royal. New France already had a governor at Quebec.

Father Hermadore offered no details, but obliquely hinted that he, through Manny the Portygee, had been obliged to pull a string here and there to get this Grandfontaine off his back, and that relations between Havre Aubert and Port Royal were not all sugar and spice. And, Father Hermadore had no idea what possible "king's business" Grandfontaine might have with the late Jules Marcoux of Morning River. He promised to look in upon his homeward-bound trip from Boston, and was helped aboard when the boat came for him. He stood in the stern and waved his crucifix until he was out of sight beyond the estuary. Those at Morning River Farm called "Bon voyage" after him. Elzada had taught the boys that much French, anyway.

8

Governor Grandfontaine is welcomed at Morning
River, but declines an invitation to anchor for
the night

When the high and mighty Grandfontaine (Ah! Father
Hermadore had done him justice!)—when the high and
mighty *Governor* Grandfontaine did come to Morning
River, his visit was brief and his business a fizzle. It was
all a big mistake. Well, Jules Marcoux was long gone
and a letter to him certainly proved that somebody was
misinformed. As Elzada had guessed, Grandfontaine had
found the name of Jules Marcoux in the archives at Port
Royal, left over from the days of Claude de la Tour,
and assuming the man still lived had written to him.
There would be something he wanted from Jules—

64

information, a favor—what might it be? Norman was marking a board to be cut and Cap'n 'Lon was holding the pattern, when the arriving vessel blew its signal gun down the estuary. Looking up in wonder, they went to the open door of the shop, giving on the wharf. A schooner. "She's French," said Cap'n 'Lon. "Maybe it's that joker looking for Marcoux."

The arrival of "Governor" Grandfontaine was less dignified than His Excellency might have wished. The puff of smoke from the signal gun was holding its shape, as there was no movement of air in the estuary that afternoon. Lacking air, the schooner had lost steerage-way and sat helpless in the slack tide. Norman pushed off a skiff and rowed down, coming alongside to discover Governor Grandfontaine in full uniform, splendid and magnificent, ready to make the grand arrival. It was not a time to be becalmed. "Welcome to Morning River," called Norman, and the governor turned to the sailors behind him with the evident question, "Are we in the right place?" One of the sailors came to the rail and said something of which Norman got only the word, the name, "Marcoux." Norman nodded, and spread his hands in a gesture of come-aboard. Cap'n 'Lon, from the wharf, greatly enjoyed watching the peacock descend a ladder—looking as if he'd never seen a ladder before. He bounced in a heap in Norman's skiff and would have swamped it except that Norman threw his weight the other way just in time. While Norman was rowing to the wharf, Cap'n 'Lon went up to the house and brought Elzada. That Jules Marcoux was no longer around was soon communicated, and this news changed everything. The governor had expected to find Jules, and Jules was the man he wanted to see. He certainly had not expected Englishmen, and he showed his uneasiness at talking with an Englishwoman who spoke French. The governor was uncomfortable. "Is there something we can do in his absence?" Elzada asked. "May we offer hospitality?"

He *was* flustered. "No, no. Nothing. Nothing at all." But, perhaps, did she know the distance to Pentagoët?

Elzada turned to 'Lon. "He wants to know how far to The Bagaduce."

"Thirty-forty miles—that's a guess."

Elzada said, "Vers dix lieues."

So now they knew Governor Grandfontaine had been expecting Jules Marcoux to help him with information about Pentagoët. It was comical to think that Jules never knew anything about Pentagoët anyway. Cap'n 'Lon now made a gesture, pointing down the estuary and then sweeping his arm around to the right. Then he pointed overland, about north-northwest. Governor Grandfontaine repeated the movements, nodded, and said, "Merci."

'Lon said, "Tell him when the tide turns he can drift down to anchor for the night—he'll beach out where he is." But the governor gratefully refused hospitality and asked to be returned to his schooner. Elzada sensed his uneasiness, even embarrassment. His information had been bad. He did commend Elzada on her French, but asked no questions as to how she acquired it. He looked at—carefully studied—the two homes, the barns, the boat shop, the mill. As he stepped into Norman's skiff, he said to Elzada, "I ask your pardon, I did not know."

Norman rowed him down the estuary and he gained the deck of his schooner with a bit more grace than he had shown in the descent. The tide turned soon, and the schooner slowly began to drift towards the ocean. Then a whisper of a breeze reached the sails, and the signal gun was touched off again in farewell. Presumably a course would be set for Pentagoët, The Bagaduce—the Shining City of the Bashaba. The schooner would get there before dark.

The Commandant of Port Royal, His Excellency the Governor of Acadia, had visited Morning River.

9

How winter came to Morning River, and how
Mavryck came in April, and about the trout and the
fiddlehead ferns

Father Hermadore did stop on his way back from Boston, but only overnight. He said nothing about his business there, and nothing about meeting with a very ugly
man to discuss port wine. The weather had been kind.
He was interested that "Governor" Grandfontaine had
called, and agreed there was probably a connection with
Pentagoët. He recalled that there had been some talk
about reviving the old French fort at Pentagoët, if only
as a buffer against the English. If that was the idea, then
Jules Marcoux might have helped. Yes. Then Father
Hermadore sailed for Havre Aubert the next morning,

waving his crucifix until he was out of sight. The next thing that happened at Morning River was winter.

Elzada loved the Morning River winters. After the gardens had been taken care of and the sugar maples on the hill had burned themselves out in a blaze of fall foliage, the nights would come on cool and blankets had to be brought from the chests. Norman took his sloop down in good season and moored her so she wouldn't be frozen in, and one night soon after the estuary would show ice along the edges. Later, ice would clog the estuary, and the tides would churn it into pieces that, sooner or later, would go out with a tide so new ice might freeze. Life turned indoors in winter, and the two kitchens at Morning River were kept warm with wood fires on their hearths. In one or the other of the kitchens Elzada and Nora would stitch and patch and mend—the weaving and spinning had been done in warmer weather. Norman had made a stone fireplace of his own design in what was now called "the bucket end" of the boat shop, and by hanging sailcloth he held the heat enclosed. The other end of the boat shop stayed cold, and wasn't used in winter. So he and 'Lon had their doghouse and kept either busy or amused. Some of the bed chambers in both houses had fireplaces, but sleeping in warm bedrooms was a luxury for the long future. Instead, there were homespun blankets, puffs, quilts, and comfortables that absorbed, retained, and returned the natural body heat that a healthy human generates for his own comfort after a hearty supper and a good flip. On arising from a night's rest in a cold bedroom, one retreated to the kitchen, where a fire had been mulling all night in the fireplace and there was a suggestion of comfort. A stir with a poker, a few dry sticks of wood, and why should anybody complain?

The animals, snug, got their care from 'Lon and Norman and the boys, and the boys were expected to keep the kitchen woodboxes full. On good days the boys would go with 'Lon and Norman with the horses or steers for logs and firewood. Lunches were packed for that and Elzada and Nora would be alone until twilight. But the lesson sessions were kept with the boys, and this winter Elzada had taken Father Hermadore's advice and put them on French. Ah, bay, say, day, ay, eff— and when she started them she got a lump in her throat about Marie-Paule and her own girlhood grammar lessons. And now the boys were into algebra, too. And they had taken over the snares in the swamp. Then the boys were fun at the regular Wednesday night parties with roasted apples and games on the floor, and maybe a recitation. Cap'n 'Lon was teaching them to bend and splice, and on some Wednesday evenings the boys would make him beckets for his buckets. And there was one Wednesday night that winter when a vicious snowstorm swung in from the ocean and when it was time for the Kincaids to go home, not many steps away, Norman thought it was too much. So Nora and the boys spent the night at the big house while Norman waded down to keep the fire alive on the hearth. He didn't go to bed that night—slept on the floor by the fireplace. That was the wildest storm in Elzada's memory, and morning brought a sunrise of majestic beauty—bright, blinding brilliance on a world of white. Deep white. Not a breath of wind after the storm, and beyond the drifted snow an ocean quiet and blue to the end of forever. But there came—there always comes—the climb up "March Hill," and it was time to tap the sugar maples again, and Morning River was showing patches of water through the ice and snow. Then the ice left the estuary for good and a run of smelts appeared by the wheel at the mill. One morning a flock of black ducks coasted in and spent a tide bobbing for food right by the wharf. Winter wasn't such a long time, was it?

And of late years, if you wanted something to look forward to, there was always that magic day in April when the chandlery ketch of Townes Estate—always trim and tidy and looking new with bright white sails—perked up the estuary precisely on a coming tide and James Mavryck stepped to the wharf for his annual trout hunt. He would turn to take his luggage and gear from a sailor wearing the almost-too-too-magnificent Townes Estate house uniform, and then wave the ketch back to sea. The crew would be on their own for two weeks, when the ketch would return to take Mavryck back to Boston. Mavryck had a Townes Estate uniform, too, but he never wore it at Morning River—woolen breeks and shirt, and a leather jerkin for him. This was his holiday from the management of Townes Estate. His arrival called for a ceremony.

'Lon and Norman would meet him at the wharf and help with his effects toward the house. Elzada would be in the kitchen at the big house to bid him welcome thricefold and say, "Que tu es joli, mon cher! Chaque an tu deviens plus agréable!" Then, "Voici un flip!" Then Nora would appear to say the fiddleheads were ready and waiting, and behind her would be the boys with an alder pole fitted with line and hook—a smidgen of salt pork invitingly disposed upon the hook. It was Mavryck's insistence that he be permitted to find the trout that would accompany the fiddleheads. He and the boys would head for the pool below the upper falls—close enough to the big house so the sound of dropping water was a constant symphony to life there. So soon after ice-out there would be little time needed for finding trout, and the boys had a basket for bringing them back. And plenty of bait.

Fiddleheads! The swamp was a fiddlehead farm. The tightly coiled shoots of fern, resembling the neck on a violin, are tender and sweet, with their own flavor, for but a few days each spring. Once the coil unfolds and the stem begins to make a frond, the moment is gone. Steam them, anoint them with butter, salt them sparingly, and add a drop of cider vinegar! That the fiddlehead fern coincides with the first seasonal feed of brook trout must have been arranged in the original divine plan for happiness. Trout, and a pan of Nora's hot buttermilk biscuits. Nora had the touch.

The eastern brook trout was originally a sea run fish. All along The Maine and even to Greenland, every tidal stream had its annual spawning run of trout, coming up from salt water into the fresh. Like the true Atlantic salmon, and unlike many fish of that family, the eastern brook trout spawns in the fall, so is "in season" in the spring. But a million years ago, the brook trout, also like its cousin the salmon, became "landlocked," and many would come up to spawn and to stay, never to return to the ocean. It is right after the ice leaves the brooks in April that the descendants of these prehistoric lingerers lie in wait for the unwary angler, and will strike with ferocious hunger at any reasonable offering. Upon being invited to breakfast, however, the trout displays reluctance, and has been known to protest until he makes his escape. There have been those, including James Mavryck, who pursue the trout mostly to test his muscle, but all such agree there is merit in fetching one home to go with the fiddleheads. Mavryck and the boys were not long at the pool.

Elzada pulled on her boots, for she would walk down to the Kincaid house for breakfast. Not only *for* breakfast, but to make breakfast—in this annual vernal ceremony it was her privilege to lean over the hearth and fry trout until Mavryck, and everybody else, called quits.

10

*This time Mavryck combines business and pleasure,
and there is conjecture about what may be going on*

On his April visits to hound the trout, Mavryck left the
business in Boston, but this time he made an exception
after he saw the letter to Jules Marcoux from Governor
Grandfontaine. And after he learned that Grandfontaine had been to The Bagaduce. This led to a recitation
of affairs. Mavryck read the letter from Grandfontaine
twice, tilted his long lantern jaw south by east, tapped
the paper against his knee, and said, "I never knew Jules
Marcoux."

"He was a sweet, lovable, dear little Frenchman who
amounted to my second father. He had a heart bigger
than a tub and he knew more than God—except per-

haps God could speak a little English. He and my father lived and worked together, and did everything you see here—houses, barns, mill, shop, gardens, everything. Jules never spoke a cross word and never did a bad thing. When that letter came, for a split second I thought maybe Jules was still here and I could hand it to him. I tried not to cry, because I didn't want to see me crying over another man. Jules got us our French deed and brought back the fake birth certificate that shows my father was born in France."

That Grandfontaine had found Jules Marcoux in the old records at Port Royal was all right, but why was Grandfontaine looking for such in the old records? Whatever prompted him, he certainly believed that Jules would be useful. Elzada said, "Father Hermadore doesn't think much of Grandfontaine."

Mavryck was careful to keep his flip mug from spilling when he shot his weight up off the stool and stood. "Father Hermadore? Do you know Father Hermadore?"

Elzada and 'Lon looked at each other. So it *was* their very own James Mavryck that the priest had seen in Boston. On wine business for Manny. Elzada said, "Yes, and we're acquainted with his M. LaManche, too."

Mavryck sat down.

Elzada said, "We sure do know Father Hermadore. He married us. He was here last summer—said he was going to Boston on business, to see a man named LaManche who isn't too pretty to look at."

Mavryck stared into his flip mug, swirled the mug, waggled his great head, and said, "I think we've got our arse in a sling."

Cap'n 'Lon offered, " 'Zadie, I think you're about to hear some things you don't know!"

Mavryck continued to swirl and stare, and then he'd sip, and then he'd waggle his head. When he started to speak he would pause and swirl again. Then he said, "It doesn't fit together. But it has to fit together! Do you know if this Father Hermadore connects you with Townes Estate?"

"Not for sure. But he could. Manny the Portygee might have told him."

"Who's Manny the Portygee?"

Cap'n 'Lon filled in. "Old friend and partner of mine when I was at sea. He used Father Hermadore for a front, and still does. Manny went to the Magdalens and brought Hermadore here to marry us, but I'm not sure Manny ever knew about Townes Estate and Elzada. But Hermadore did say he was going to Boston about Manny's wines."

Mavryck said, "Port wines. We did business. Good future in port wines. But he said he talked for somebody in Portugal—nothing about this Manny. But I still can't put things together. Can you trust this Manny?"

"To the hilt, and a thousand times I have. And can we trust this damned priest?"

"I see now that I've got to. The whole point in doing business with Hermadore was that, in a way, he was supposed to cheat us. How do you trust somebody about to cheat you?"

Elzada said, "Father Hermadore isn't about to cheat me."

James Mavryck permitted his version of a wry smile to flit at his lips, but he kept it from bursting into a catastrophe. He sipped his flip before saying, "Maybe you'll find it profitable to let him."

"And why don't you," said Cap'n 'Lon, "tell us whatever the hell it is we ought to know?"

And that led to something of a recitation.

The Indian troubles had simmered down, but that left the Bostons without many friends, and not too many people, up along the coast towards The Maine. Same thing happened to the French, but not for just the same reasons, and between The Bagaduce and Ste. Croix there wouldn't be more than a couple of dozen families, if that. Big trouble was that people on this side didn't pay close attention to what went on in Europe, and the important people over there had their minds on about everything except colonies. Take Governor Temple, for whom James Mavryck had no use—he'd been running wrong every time he lifted a foot. Governor of Massachusetts, he got all excited about New Amsterdam and decided it was his duty to send down an expedition and take the place back for the English. Never belonged to England anyway. So a fleet of four warships with five hundred men aboard shows up at New Amsterdam to find out that King Charlie had just made a treaty with the Dutch, and Temple was looking plain silly. But you give a foolish man authority and an army, and he's going to do something, so Temple decides to cover his embarrassment by wreaking horrible slaughter on the wicked French. Somebody told him the French were up to no good down east. So the four warships and the soldiers show up at The Bagaduce with orders to reduce the fort, disperse the French, and set up a truckhouse for trading with the Indians. The French had no business being there anyway. But when the ships arrive at The Bagaduce, what do you know . . . ? The old fort was all grown up with bushes, there hadn't been a Frenchman there in years, and the Indians were all back in the woods. Big victory. But then Temple learns that King Charles had just made a treaty with Louis Quatorze, too, and that now Acadia belongs to France. Temple's having his boys at The Bagaduce violated the treaty and was an act of open war, even if there was nobody there to shoot at, and it seemed as if Temple couldn't win. But with good Boston logic, he decided King Charles and King Louis didn't know their own business, and since he had The Bagaduce he might as well keep it.

"So our very good question is," said Mavryck, "who owns The Bagaduce?"

"So who does?"

"Well, France. Temple's problem is that he doesn't have a man in Boston with wit enough to skin a beaver, and nobody smart enough to want to come to The Maine. So his grip on The Bagaduce is just that he says it's his. So it's both and neither, and that's where the wine comes in."

"By God, you're right!" said Elzada. "I can see just as plain as the nose on your face that this is where the wine comes in!"

"You leave my nose alone. You don't know about the wine, and I'm about to tell you. Some years ago we— you—sewed up the Lübeck wine business. Good deal, and it's paid. I never understood why, but a long time ago the Frenchmen decided their red Bordeaux wines were improved by a sea voyage. So they made a deal with the city of Lübeck, way over the other side of Germany, and Lübeck goes into the business of storing the wines after they've made the trip. Gives the wines a rest. Don't ask me—I don't have the faintest. Now, there's been a funny thing about Bordeaux—way back in the time of one of the Henry kings there was a marriage that made that part of France a dominion of England. Fact. All the Frenchmen suddenly became Englishmen with all the rights and privileges. Bordeaux wines, but not wines from other parts of France, got into England duty free, and ever since then the upright and honest Englishman likes his Bordeaux claret. Patriotic drink. But the claret has to go to Lübeck, and with all the hassles in Europe there comes about a shortage of boats. The Townes Estate steps in. Boats, we have. If it hadn't been for you, Mrs. Plaice, the English people would have died of thirst. So we're not all that much in the wine business, but we handle a lot of wine, which is what the question was."

Cap'n 'Lon said, "I think there's a bottle or two of Bordeaux claret down cellar—I picked up a case of it one time somewhere. Maybe if I get a bottle we can understand what we're talking about."

"Don't bother—flip suits me."

Elzada said, "So what's with The Bagaduce?"

"Oh, that's right—The Bagaduce. Well, right now we've got a place handy for everything that's both French and English, and maybe neither one, and there's ways to make a kind of a Lübeck out of it. Bring wines here for a little rest, say ten or fifteen minutes, and then move them along as seems helpful. Nobody except us needs to know what's afoot. You see, I was hoping to work Father Hermadore along for a trial run, to see how things come out, and maybe work port wine into a healthy competition with claret. We'll never get a hand onto claret, but Father Hermadore tells me we can buy and sell port—not just carry it. How would this friend of yours, Manny the Portygee, be in the port wine business?"

"Simple enough. We didn't know until Father Hermadore told us, but about the time I gave up the sea Manny went back to Portugal. Got back his old family lands. Vineyards."

"All right," Mavryck said. "I see how some of this fits together. Maybe some more of it will. I guess our big worry is what this Grandfontaine has in mind over at The Bagaduce."

Elzada had an afterthought. "Funny that all the time this Bagaduce place sits over there and we don't hear about it, know anything about it, and never go there."

"I think you'll hear about it," said Mavryck.

11

Norman doesn't catch a fish, but they have a good
look at the city of Bashaba—which was not too
impressive

On the third morning of his visit, after breakfast, Mavryck said, "Anybody can eat just about so many trout."
Which is true. After three-four trout breakfasts in a row,
ham-and-eggs will sound fine. With home-fries. Nora
said she had been planning on ham and eggs. So having
no trout to fry this morning, Elzada was sitting at the
table with everybody except Nora, and she said, "Why
do you think Father Hermadore might cheat us?"

"I didn't know you knew him. I got a letter from him,
we met and we talked, and I thought I might use him.
Kind of involved, but it might have worked out. But if

he's a friend, that's that. I had in mind letting him ride a cargo of claret around and see if anybody caught him. Sounding out a tax scheme. Might be Father Hermadore could be cheaper than passing customs. Is the man really a priest?"

"Oh, sure. I have an idea he's a good one. He got rid of his church long ago, thanks to Manny, but he keeps his hand in with a fake parish at the Magdalens. And, he's thick with Manny, so he isn't in pain. How much do *you* know about Manny?"

"Nothing except what you tell me. Hermadore gave me to understand he's a count or a seigneur, or something, in Portugal, but he didn't tell me he's your Manny the Portygee."

"Well, he is—and that's good news. For years we thought Manny had drowned. 'Lon wouldn't believe that, because he didn't believe a Portygee would drown. Said Manny was too good a sailor. Now Father Hermadore says Manny is planning to come back to The Maine. He had a place, you know, over on the island." She pointed over Nora's breakfast table, across at Outer Razor.

Mavryck said, "Maybe things do fit together after all. But I couldn't figure it out at first. And I'm wondering if it wouldn't be smart to make a little look-around visit over to The Bagaduce?"

So the next morning, on Cap'n 'Lon's sloop *Morning Star*, off went 'Lon, Norman, and Mavryck to take a look at The Bagaduce. Cap'n 'Lon deferred to Norman, who took the tiller, and he and James Mavryck made themselves comfortable in the warm sun, supported by several buckets that included, along with lunches, several bottles of Bordeaux claret that had, indeed, been down cellar. The two Kincaid boys had wanted to come along, but Mavryck talked them out of it on the grounds that they might run into some kind of trouble not foreseen. Norman picked up a quartering breeze and the sloop was soon out of sight from Morning River.

"I don't have the foggiest idea of what we'll find," said Cap'n 'Lon. Norman said, "I've never even thought about heading in that direction."

Mavryck said, "I have something of a vague idea. Back along I sent a crew up to make some maps, and all the reports were good. Beautiful place. Back from the ocean, but deep water. Scenery enough for everybody. French had a fort at one time, but it's gone. Just a few earthworks left. Used to be some buildings. Now and then Indians, but they come and go. The surveyors said they were pleasant enough; took an interest in the maps and wanted to help. Spoke a little English, but knew more French."

As they moved along, Norman rigged a baited hook and put a line overboard. He let the line run out a good distance before he secured it, and then there was conjecture as to what might be caught. Too early for mackerel. Probably not grounds for cod and haddock. On a boat, people keep their eyes on a line astern, hoping to see it tighten. This one didn't. It dragged all day and nothing touched it. The sky was blue. The water was blue. The sun was high. The air was warm. The sloop, made from Norman's "Kincaid Pattern," moved sedately, using every whisper of air. Beyond the creak of rigging and the swish of water at the bow, there wasn't a sound until Mavryck, lulled asleep, began to snore. Mavryck snored with a difference. He would start one deep down within his substance, culturing it for an ascent, and then would fetch it upward with rising inflection until, reaching at last its peak, it (Cap'n 'Lon told Elzada later) "it busted." The sun was still east of south when Mavryck, reacting to his own noise, jerked alive with a great shudder, looked about, and reached in one of the buckets to find a cork puller. The prolonged meal was still in progress when Norman sang out, "Ship ahead—starboard!"

It was the same vessel that had brought Governor Grandfontaine to Morning River, looking for Jules Marcoux. She was close inshore, but tied or anchored they couldn't be sure at that distance. They presumed the inlet to be The Bagaduce. No people could be seen, but Norman spied a wisp of smoke rising from the shore—behind the boat. "You're sure she's French?" asked Mavryck.

"She's French," said Cap'n 'Lon. "Same one brought Grandfontaine in his monkey suit. Real class. Think we should move closer in?"

"No need to, really. I see enough from right here. French ship, some kind of camp. Would the smoke be from Indians?"

"We can go in and see," said Norman. "If they don't want us around we can come about and be out of sight before they could shake out a line. Why don't we?"

"Norm's right," said Cap'n 'Lon. "That vessel didn't have a full working crew anyway. They made right up into a flat-arse calm at Morning River and didn't know what happened. We could get back home before they could pick their killick. French always make good sailors until they have to sail something. Elzada says even her Jules Marcoux used to twist his sloop around a couple of times just raising the gaff."

Mavryck said, "It might be they won't mind us anyway—things are supposed to be quiet these days. Why'n't we go in so we can see if there's buildings—a wharf, maybe?"

It turned out the Frenchmen didn't mind. They stood on the shore and watched the sloop pass. The smoke came from a campfire, with a couple of tents close by. There was no wharf; the ship was anchored, but just offshore enough to swing. Deep water close in. When Mavryck said, "That's good enough," Norman turned the sloop homeward.

"Good harbor," said Cap'n 'Lon. "They don't beach out there twice a day, the way we do at Morning River."

"That survey crew said that," said Mavryck. "Said it wouldn't take any time to make a pier. And good holding ground, all along. Your Father Hermadore said The Bagaduce is the best harbor along The Maine. He'd had use of it now and then. I have an idea we'll get to use it, too."

Cap'n 'Lon looked back at the French vessel anchored as if in full possession, and he said, "If Governor Temple thinks The Bagaduce is his, what is Governor Grandfontaine thinking?"

Mavryck smiled his complicated smile where his jaw went out of joint and he had the same thing as a convulsion to get it back in line. "They're both thinking to make a penny, and so am I. Now, the way we're going—do we get back for supper or shall I look into the claret bucket again?"

Since Mavryck was already twisting the corkscrew, Cap'n 'Lon saw no need to reply, but reached across with his mug. The buckets still had food, so supper back at Morning River was not critical. The afternoon breeze was offshore and Norman set sail to catch it in a good chance along. So the whole stretch of the land ran

from bow to stern on the left hand. Mavryck gestured
with his mug of claret at the long spruce-tree shoreline.
"That's Norumbega!" he said.

Norumbega was beautiful.

12

To the east'ard, pleasuring, and Cap'n 'Lon fails to
burn his fingers when he opens a bake

After the ketch came to take Mavryck back to Boston,
summer ran along until Nora and Elzada, one day, were
packing down wild raspberries for winter. The buckets
that Cap'n 'Lon made in the boat shop were just right
for that. A layer of berries and a layer of sugar until the
bucket was full, sugar on top, and then a round cover
that fitted inside the bucket and pressed down on the
sugar. Put a stone on top to make the pressure. The
berries came out in the winter just like the summertime,
and the juice made a special treat for the boys—or for
anybody else, for that matter. Half a cup of juice and
half a cup of water—cold water. Marie-Paule used to

say that was good for an upset stomach, but it was good anyway. Cap'n 'Lon, having no part in the preserving, was on a stool by the window making beckets for his buckets. "Idiot work," he called it. But every bucket needed two beckets. Take a length of rope apart so you have three strands. Then lay one strand onto itself, three times around in a circle, and you have a ring with neither beginning nor end. Leastways, you can't see any ends. A handle. And he heard Elzada say to Nora, "I've never been to the east'ard."

He said, "What brought on that remark?"

"Well, I never have. Jules Marcoux used to take me jigging for mackerel, and when we got to the end of Outer Razor he'd turn and come back. Farthest east I've ever been, and I can see the place right here from my window." Cap'n 'Lon idled his hands for a minute, stretching his fingers, and he said, "You got a big problem. If you want to go down east, all you do is write to Jim Mavryck. Take two-three days going, and two-three for Jim to jump—and what do I see? Do you see what I see?"

"What do you see?" It was Nora who asked.

"I see a boat coming in with smart sailors in Townes uniforms, and they'd have orders to sail you any place you want to go. My gawd, 'Zadie! You own more boats than anybody! Why don't you order up a fleet or two? I'd like to go along. I won't touch a line, sass a sailor, find fault with the grub."

Elzada put a wooden cover into a bucket, pushed down, and said, "I've been thinking about Father Hermadore and Manny, about things going on. I've been wondering about the Magdalens. Curiosity. Why don't we go?"

Cap'n 'Lon said, "We can leave right away, or put it

both were built to Norman's pattern. Nor-man's would be more comfortable. So 'Lon and Nor-
The last time—really, thethe *Madrigal* to the Islands to sell her.sugar ships, a bit ofwho'd had his own command—trip. Norman said,"Why'n't we lash some buckets on deck and you see ifyou can get rid of the damned things? Then maybe Ican turn around in my own shop without going outdoors.""You sound like Mavryck—do something to pay forthe trip."Any time is a good time, but raspberry time is fine.
There is always a chance that fog will close in on The
Maine until September, but fog wasn't about to bother
this kind of a trip. 'Lon and Elzada didn't have to go
when they didn't want to go, and Elzada set the mood
by saying, "Our trip to the Islands wasn't exactly one,
so let's make this our honeymoon."

THE WINES OF PENTAGOËT|90
THE WINES OF PENTAGOËT|90

"Good!" said Cap'n 'Lon. "Now, let's see—just what is it that people do on honeymoons?"

The checklist was checked and double checked, and with a skiff in tow the sloop drifted down the estuary on a forenoon tide. The Kincaids waved them off, and Elzada waved back, but Cap'n 'Lon didn't wave until he had the gaff set. The sail rippled, caught a breeze, and 'Lon steadied the tiller. Now he waved. There was a pause to check the packetbutt, which was empty, and then the sloop was at sea. "Where to?"

Elzada spread her hands. "Doesn't matter—show me things I ought to see. I'd like to see the Magdalens."

"Not much, really. Name is romantic, the rocks aren't. But we'll see them. Maybe we'll spend tonight at Desert Mountain—Cadillac. Mountain comes right up out of the water. All right?"

"Right as rain. You're the captain, and this is one boat I don't own."

"And don't you forget it! If I yell to jump overboard, you jump!"

"Yes, sir."

A fair westerly pushed the sloop along and for a time Cap'n 'Lon kept four and five miles offshore. The dark spruces of The Maine made an unbroken horizon to their left. Nothing showed on that horizon to indicate a home, let alone a village. Mount Cadillac crept up, and now 'Lon brought the sloop closer to land. "Used to be some French in there, back before our time." He pointed. "English drove them out. Place was called Saint Saviour."

Elzada remembered. "Right! Jules Marcoux used to tell a lot of stories about Saint Saviour. Loved to tell about the cow. The French had a cow, and when the English burned the place they stole the cow and took it to South Virginia. Then there was a priest there, too,

and they took him to South Virginia. The cow didn't
understand any English, and the priest was the only
one knew any French. They needed him to take care of
the cow. They didn't let him go back to France until
the cow died. I used to ask him why they didn't teach
the cow some English."

"I know somewhere near where Saint Saviour was.
Want to spend the night there?"

"Why not? Jules called it Saint Sauveur. Same thing."

Cap'n 'Lon wasn't sure if he found the place of Saint
Sauveur or not. It didn't matter, because the shoreline
under "les monts deserts" has cove after cove with deep
water and good shelter. He picked a cove, saying he
thought it was the right one, and before he sailed in he
baited and set a lobster trap. It settled into the water,
leaving a wooden buoy to show the place. "Maybe a
bake tomorrow," he said, and he sailed into the cove.

The jug of cream that had been stowed in the bilge
would stay cool for a few days. 'Lon brought it up after
he hove anchor and before he trimmed ship for the night,
and by the time he was ready Elzada had flips made.
He took his mug from her, touched it to hers, and said,
"Now, my fair lady—I want you to show me just what
it is that people do on honeymoons."

The sunset over Cadillac foretold a fair day, but there
was low-hanging fog in the morning. From the deck,
they could see the peak in the shining splendor of sunrise, but the shoreline was hidden. But the fog scaled
off when the sun went to work on it, and before Elzada
had the breakfast dishes cleaned there was a day to
remember spread out in all directions. Blue, blue, blue
was the ocean and sky. 'Lon went ashore in the skiff
and found a bucket of clams and some rockweed. On
the way out of the cove he hauled his lobster trap and

found five competent volunteers. He lashed the trap back into the skiff, adjusted sail, and "Where to?"

"Won't be easy to find another place cozy as that one," Elzada said.

"Don't bet on it. From here to Fundy coves like that come fifteen to the dozen. I have in mind one at Pleasant Bay. Not far, we can dawdle along. Manny and I used to go into a cove there and buy pogey oil from a Frenchman. We'd leave ten barrels, and come back after he filled them. Used to squeeze every pogey by hand, I think. Took the stuff to Salem where they made paint. Didn't mean anything at the time, but we sold it to John Townes. We cheated the Frenchman and Townes cheated us, and everybody was happy. If the Frenchman's still there, you can talk to him—Manny and I never could. Lived with a squaw. But not the same squaw every time."

Before the sun was high, 'Lon ran closer to shore, looking for a place. He anchored off a short sandy beach flanked by garnet-red ledges, and ran the skiff up so Elzada stepped ashore dry-footed. They carried blankets, wine, biscuits, and a package of bilge-cool butter above high tide mark. Elzada broke off some sea lavender and stuck it in her hair. Then, while 'Lon scouted for firewood she picked stones from under a ledge and arranged them in the little magic circle first laid on the shores of The Maine five thousand years ago by people now forgotten except for their little circles of stones. On the circle of stones 'Lon laid his kindlings. A pinch of gunpowder on the tow in the tinderbox, and a quick, sharp strike of the steel against the flint. The gunpowder flared, the tow glowed, and 'Lon blew a flame. The bits of birch bark caught, and then they piled their firewood on in a heap. The stones would get hot, and one more "bake" in the history of the lobster would be under way. They opened a bottle of wine, stood on the beach waiting for the stones to heat, and looked at the ocean.

'Lon cut some spruce limbs to be used like a broom, and when the fire reduced itself to ashes and embers he swept the hot stones clean. A flavor of evergreen pitch resulted when the heat got to the limbs. Elzada dumped the bucket of clams onto the hot stones, and 'Lon laid on his lobsters. Over all went the rockweed from Saint Sauveur to hold down the steam. "Can you wait?" he asked.

"Barely. but I do want to see you burn your fingers. It isn't a bake if fingers don't get burned. Jules always made the bakes when I was little, and he would forever burn his fingers when he opened one. No matter that he'd done it before. No matter how much we warned him. He'd always jump back with a silent cuss-word and stick his fingers in his mouth. It goes with a bake. Can't you use a stick and not get burned?"

"The steam fools you. First bake I saw, an Indian did it to show me how. He was a wild one. Spoke better English than I did, right out of London. Worked there ten years making wheels in a wagon factory, but didn't like it and came home to Canada. He said getting burned by the steam is ritualistic—the very word he used—and explains the Red Man's disregard for pain. I can hear him now, a Cockney Micmac. Went by the name of Fortescue."

"Use a stick, anyhow."

He did, and spared himself a steaming. The clams and lobsters were perfectly cooked, and didn't last long. Afterwards, they cleaned away surplus seafood juices and residual butter in the usual manner—they swam out to the sloop and back. Then they lay on the blankets in the sun. The circle of stones was cool and the afternoon on the wane when they rowed out and 'Lon got the sloop under way for Pleasant Bay.

13

Improbably, the physical dimensions of King
Richard of the Lion's Heart remind of a
cunner chowder

Except that he had a pleasant time at a comfortable place,
Governor Grandfontaine didn't do much that summer
at Pentagoët. According to what Mavryck reported later,
he left nothing in the way of buildings, but there were
bare spots where tents had been set up long enough to
kill the grass. Firewood had been cut and burned. The
considerable history about the doings at Quebec and at
Port Royal offer no details about Pentagoët that year—
just that Commandant Grandfontaine visited the place
in an effort to frustrate English exploitation. Luckily,
Grandfontaine had no confrontation with Governor

Temple of Massachusetts, who was telling everybody that he was keeping the French from exploiting The Bagaduce. The two seem not to have hindered each other. So while Elzada and 'Lon were anchored that afternoon at Pleasant Bay, Governor Grandfontaine passed to the east'ard after several months at Pentagoët. Because Cap'n 'Lon had his sails down and the sloop blended into the shoreline, Governor Grandfontaine, or his lookout, didn't make a sighting, but Elzada and 'Lon saw the Grand-fontaine vessel highlighted by the setting sun and watched her pass. "She's the one came looking for Jules," 'Lon said. "Same one we saw at The Bagaduce. Could be we'll see her again at Port Royal."

"How long before Port Royal?"

"Better than a day. Maybe three days. No hurry. We don't need to put in there until we're after supplies. We ought to stop at Grand Manan, and at Ste. Croix, and there's an Indian village along here somewhere I'd like to find again. The chief used to take a barrel of rum and a barrel of molasses every trip, whether I was gone three weeks or three months." But Cap'n 'Lon should never have conjectured about time. He knew better. He knew how a fog can settle in and close out the world, and one did. And he knew, too, about the tides and cross-chops of the Bay of Fundy. Three days? They didn't move out of Pleasant Bay for three days.

After they watched the Grandfontaine vessel pass, the sun set and the night was bright with stars. The afternoon thermal stir of air eased off with the sun, and the anchorage was as still as a basin of water. Not a cloud. But they awoke next morning to a lost world. A dense sea fog had settled around them, hugging and clinging. The shore, not fifty yards away, couldn't be seen—Elzada felt eyestrain as she tried to look. As she peered, 'Lon said, "You may be looking to sea!" Lines dripped; the deck and canvas were wet. The air was warm and held moisture just short of a drizzle. 'Lon said, "Only way to find shore is look at the anchor line. Tide should be going, and the prow will point ashore. Want to climb forward and lean over for a look?"

So they stayed there. A fogbound day offshore on a boat can become dreary. Elzada had some books—Mavryck had brought a box in April. She brought a couple up from the cabin, arranged herself against the tiller post, and began to look at them. 'Lon got out a fishline. He cut a very small gobbet from their slab of salt pork and then carefully replaced the wrapper and put the pork back in its hamper. Watching him over her book, Elzada asked, "Just going to catch one?"

"Well, now—I thought I had things figured. If there's nothing here, I don't need more bait. If there is something here, I use the first fish to bait the others. And if I do catch a mess of cunners, we'll have salt pork for a chowder."

"Cunners are the very hell to peel."

"But they make top-notch chowder."

"None better. Jules Marcoux showed me how to skin them."

"If I catch any, I'll watch you skin them."

"Jules always said he taught me to skin them so he wouldn't have to."

'Lon let the line run through his fingers until the lead hit bottom. Not quite four fathoms. Then he raised the sinker about three feet, so he wouldn't be fishing on the bottom. Almost at once he got a response. "Cunner," he said. The cunner isn't a big fish and he doesn't strike at bait. He nibbles. You have to jerk at once. You catch cunners on the nibble; not between nibbles. On his third jerk, Cap'n 'Lon brought up a cunner. He slapped the fish against the cheeserind so it went limp, and then with his sheath knife cut away a fillet of flesh. Now he had bait for a chowder. Elzada closed her book and went below to get a pan, a pot, a knife, and some cornmeal. And as fast as 'Lon brought up a cunner, she dressed it. The way Jules had shown her. A little cut under one gill to start the skin, then with some cornmeal between the fingers to counteract the cunner's slipperiness, rip away the skin to the tail. Then the other side. Now take away two fillets of pure meat, and wait for the next cunner. She tossed the skins and the bones into a bucket—they would bait the lobster trap the next time. When she had the pan heaped with meat, 'Lon wound his line. She gave the pan of meat and the pot to 'Lon with, "Here you go, Cook!"

They cleaned their hands in sea water, and 'Lon went below to start the brazier and begin the chowder. Elzada went back to her book. When he came up she said, "I know how the shore lies." She pointed. "I heard a crow." It was the only intrusion of sound all day. So catching and dressing the cunners took up some of the day, and after a little while 'Lon said, "What's the book?"

"Some chronicles. Old history. This one's about Richard of the Lion's Heart. Done by somebody who knew him in his own time. Seems he wasn't all myth and legend, puffed up to be a hero. He was real stuff. Says he had—here, let me read . . . it says he had the valor of Hector, the magnanimity of Achilles, he was no whit inferior to Alexander, or less than Roland, with the tongue of Nestor and the prudence of Ulysses."

"Quite a rooster!"

"Says he was lofty in stature, of a shapely build, with

hair halfway between yellow and red. His limbs were straight and flexible, his arms somewhat long, better fitted than most to draw or wield the sword. He had long legs, matching the character of his whole frame."

"That's the boy went on the Crusades?"

"Same boy—King Richard the First of England."

"Whoever wrote that book wrote hogwash."

"Oh?"

"Hogwash with a capital wash. That's not King Richard. King Richard was a witty-bitty squirt. Wouldn't come up to my armpits. That joker expected his reward for writing that stuff."

"Nobody knows now who he was."

"Just as well. King Richard could walk under that boom on tippy-toe. Wearing a tall hat."

"Sounds as if you knew him personally."

"I did. Called him Dickie-boy. He was a runt."

"Not according to this book."

"Book, my eye. You don't want to believe everything you read in a book. Fellow wrote that book was being nice to the king, and probably got made a duke. When I was a boy, before I left England to come here and get fogbound with a beautiful bookworm, somebody took me to a castle somewhere and I saw the suit of armor that Richard the Lion-Hearted wore when he fought the Turks. I was just a sprout, but I was already too big to get into that armor. King Richard was a runt. I've heard in those days everybody was a runt. Anybody five feet tall was a giant. All I know is, I saw that armor and it was made for a midget."

It was, Elzada thought, a little disconcerting to be fogbound with a husband who knew more about King Richard than the historians. She said, "All right, but it spoils the story. King Richard stands tall, a man with Alexander and Ulysses and Roland, and now you've cut him down."

"Well, he shouldn't have left his old armor hanging around. And come to think of it—maybe Alexander was a runt, too. My guess is those old legends about big heroes are a whole lot like a cunner chowder. The longer you stew one, the better it gets. Are you in a hurry to eat?"

14

Port Royal; and Elzada understands why Jules
Marcoux never told her about the Fundy tides

The fog persisted the next morning; it pressed down
and in and around. It didn't "feel" as if it might scale
off, so there would be no sailing on today. When a crow
spoke up, Cap'n 'Lon took a direction and went ashore
in the skiff. "I'll call if I need a fix," he said, pulled, and
left Elzada to her books. She listened to the oars in the
tholepins and then heard him ship them into the skiff.
"I found it!" he called, "we've just discovered America!" The shore wasn't all that far away. He was gone
for seventeen pages of Elzada's chronicles, during which
time good King Richard the Runt slaughtered twenty-
seven hundred Saracen children, expiating their sins in

a gesture of Christian good will. "Ahoy!"

"Ahoy, yourself! Come aboard!"

She called once more before 'Lon appeared out of the fog. He passed her up a birch-bark cone of blackcap raspberries, a cluster of wild onions that reeked, some roots of Indian rhubarb, and a cluster of sea lavender. He secured the skiff astern. "There's going to be black-berries there, too, and if this fog holds they'll be ripe before we leave." But on the third day the fog lifted, as quickly and as silently as it had come. The sun was hot on the deck before they finished breakfast and the wet rigging and sails steamed. There would be an offshore breeze later—it proved to be a sustaining westerly that sped them past Englishman Bay and Machias Bay before Elzada called up that supper was ready. 'Lon lashed the tiller and they ate.

"I've seen times," he began, "that a boat could pass Fundy Bay so you could balance an egg on the tiller and it would seem to be glued. Other times . . ."

"I've heard tell," she interrupted, "that the egg on the tiller is something an old man might see once, and a good many old men never did see."

"You heard right. Fundy generally stays Fundy most of the time. And it isn't just weather. It's the tide. Everything goes hell-bent and then everything comes hell-bent, and in between you get a hullabaloo. You can sit in a fog in a quiet air, way we did last night, and a fifteen-foot tide comes and goes and you don't know it. But when you get a tide going one way, the wind another, you a third, Fundy has a way of making you take notice. So maybe we'll find out if you're a good sailor, but if you want to keep an egg handy it might balance."

"I've still got four eggs where they can't roll around, but I meant to keep them for flips."

But Fundy didn't intrude right away. There were increasing swells, which 'Lon said came from Fundy action, The sloop rode them well. Cap'n 'Lon took in some sail and moved closer inshore, looking to recognize the place of that Indian village. He found it. Elzada had never seen an Indian village, and didn't know just what to expect. A row of canoes orderly on a sandy shore, a few people among them, and a cluster of log homes with sod roofs beyond. There were some wigwams, too, their poles thrusting up from bark and skin coverings. 'Lon said the French had taught the Indians how to make the houses, and there might be a Frenchman around. When the arriving sloop was spied, the houses emptied and a line of Indians stood watching from the beach—Elzada counted thirty. Then a canoe was launched and two Indians paddled out to meet the sloop. Cap'n 'Lon greeted them with raised arm and open palm, and as they reached for the coaming he said, "Kootana?"

The two Indians looked at each other and shook their heads. One of them said, "Mort." At that, Elzada took over.

Kootana was the chief 'Lon remembered from his trading days with the *Madrigal*, the one who always took two barrels, and he was dead. He had been dead for three runs of gaspereaux. His son, Loheedar, was now chief. Loheedar had a wife—one of his wives—who was French. The two Indians in the canoe were not fluent in French, but Elzada had no trouble understanding them, and now she chanced, humble-stumble, to say the right thing. "Are we welcome? May we visit the village?" She had in mind the skiff, with 'Lon rowing ashore. But not at all! One of the Indians motioned amidships of the canoe. Before she left the sloop she excused herself and went below. From the cabin she brought the bouquet of sea lavender, hoping it would please Loheedar's French wife. Then the Indians were amused to see 'Lon hand her solicitously into the canoe— evidently squaws did not get such deference. She hunched down and the paddles dipped.

There was one Indian who remembered 'Lon from the old days. He spoke only his Passamaquoddy, but through Loheedar's French wife and Elzada he asked 'Lon about rum and molasses. Neither, this time. Elzada gave the sea lavender to the wife, who pointed at her teeth and then at her moccasins—it was good to know the delicate, spray-like blooms of the flower were not particularly esteemed as a nosegay, but could be soaked to make a cure for mouth sores and a way to tan leather. Chief Loheedar handled some French, but deferred to his wife. The two Indian wives, saying nothing, stood beside Cécile; seemed most proud of her ability as she translated. And there was a "mug up." Not a big feast as some early explorers liked to brag about when they first visited Indians, but the offering that still prevails along The Maine in neighborly sociability. A cup of hot soup that 'Lon and Elzada couldn't identify, but good, and little strips of dried and smoked meat from pigeon breasts. Delicious. Loheedar himself took a paddle and returned 'Lon and Elzada to the sloop, while everybody else stood on the sand and waved. "Good God!" Elzada said after they were back aboard their boat, "what the hell made the Bostons so all-fired mad at Indians?"

"You got your postulations askew—I read that in one of your books. What happened is that the Indians got mad at the Bostons."

"All right, but where would you go to find anybody nicer than they were? Friendly, glad to see us—and I guess nobody anywhere is any happier than they are."

'Lon said, "Notice how those two squaw wives hung on every word that Cécile said? I had a wonder about how three women got along in one bed—but those two were just as proud of her as could be. They think she's great!"

"I didn't see any envy. Makes me wonder who she was. How did she get here? Pretty girl. What would she be back in France if she hadn't wound up here?"

"No way of knowing, but here—she's queen. Every time I came here to bring old Kootana his two barrels it was like that. Treated the best, and always left with a hope to come back. Might be these Indians down this way run more to cream than some others. I'm glad I could find the place."

Then the Fundy tides did intrude. 'Lon didn't say anything as the swells began to mount, but he turned now and then to see if Elzada noticed. Just beyond Grand Manan, with an ingoing tide and a following wind, the sloop began to pitch. The pitching was soon severe. Nothing the sloop couldn't weather, and no danger, but everything had to be secured and 'Lon and Elzada were hanging on. She grinned at him. He wondered if green would show at her gills, which is a way of saying it, and if she would go below to enjoy the miseries of a Fundy afternoon. There was no great breeze, so the sloop wasn't heeled, but there was this uppy-downy. Elzada let go the coaming and reached for 'Lon's hand, to join him at the tiller. They stood braced. "I see what you mean," she said.

He said, "There's no rhythm to it."

"How long does it go on?"

"We won't live that long. It eases on the slack, and then picks up again. We'll lose it when we get behind the Passamaquoddy Islands, but it'll be waiting for us when we come out in the morning. You going to weather it?"

"Oh, sure!"

The height of a swell and the depth of the trough that followed had no constant values. Now the sloop would slide gently down a swell and ride comfortably to lift again on the next swell. But then it would go down with a bump and come up with a jerk. Then, again, it wouldn't. But running with the tide and with a following wind, the sloop wasn't long in coming behind the islands, and 'Lon found a cove and anchored for the night.

Elzada said, "Funny Jules Marcoux never told me anything about the Fundy tides. He used to come this way every so often, but he never described the tides."

"Maybe he didn't want to try. Could you describe that ride you just had to somebody who never had it?"

Then, across the bay, they came to Port Royal. They saw first the masts of the governor's schooner. She was at anchor. Then there were a good many small vessels, the harbor fleet—some on moorings and some at wharves. Then houses and other buildings, and acres of fish flakes behind them. The codfish being cured on the flakes yielded a briny smell that wafted out over the harbor as a greeting and came to Elzada and 'Lon still at a distance. One wharf had an idle side, and 'Lon came in to tie up. The wharf was covered with barrels, and on the other side some men with a shears were lowering barrels into a vessel. From a rambling building above the wharf came the knocking of coopers' mallets—brined fish were being headed up for shipment. The tide was about half. 'Lon climbed a ladder and the men at the shears nodded to him. "Can you make it?" he called down.

At his English, the men on the shears were curious and came across, arriving just as Elzada topped the ladder. Her *bonjour* won her some *b'envenus*, and thus they were welcomed to Port Royal, the capital of Acadia. When she inquired for Governor Grandfontaine, the men looked at one another and shrugged—Cap'n 'Lon got the idea they wondered why anybody would ask for *him*. Then one of them said Governor Grandfontaine had just returned from Pentagoët. "Yes, we know. He visited us on the trip."

There was really no need to ask for the governor's house—it stood out. It was the biggest at the harbor, of logs, and by the stockade. Two cannon stood by the front entrance, pointed over the harbor. A soldier stood on the porch, but he was a casual sentry, plainly bored with nothing to do. "A courtesy call on His Excellency," Elzada said, and without a challenge the sentry turned to open the door for them.

Governor Grandfontaine was completely surprised. He had on his resplendent uniform—'Lon surmised he slept in one—and except for one thing he was the exalted image of French sovereignty. That one thing was his wig—he had his wig off and it reposed alone, awkward and conspicuous on the huge polished oak desk at which he sat. He looked up from his nodding, gulped, grabbed the wig, turned back to, and arranged himself. When he turned back he seemed composed, as if every hair on his head were his very own, and he offered a welcome and his hand. But Elzada had to remind him that there had been a meeting at Morning River, when he was looking for M. Marcoux. "Ah, oui!" and he spoke over his shoulder towards a door from which came, almost immediately, an Indian woman with brandy and crystal.

They would, of course, be honored to join His Excellency for dinner, and as they helped him with his brandy he asked about matters at Morning River. He had gone there expecting French, and he was embarrassed that his information had been wrong. Elzada explained how her father and Jules Marcoux had shared the place until it gained a double nationality—being both and being neither. Then, Cap'n 'Lon asked Elzada to inquire about things at The Bagaduce.

No—he had really done nothing there. He had been sent to establish French control, but he had found nothing to control. Some Indians came and went. He hadn't seen any English. He didn't remember the day when 'Lon, Norman, and Jim Mavryck had sailed by. It was a beautiful place. But he decided he had been there long enough and came back to Port Royal. Yes, he expected that one day he would return to Pentagoët—there were plans for a garrison there and some settlements. A post with factor. Things depended. He hoped to visit Quebec soon, where he might find out more about what was expected of him at Pentagoët. Meantime, Port Royal was a lonely place and he was delighted to have company for dinner.

While he talked, Elzada recalled Father Hermadore's version—how this governor was no more than a commandant, and how he had been banished at the whim of the king's mistress. Now she wondered about this Indian woman with the brandy. And, in turn, about Loheedar's French wife. How about that? Win some, lose some. Would Governor Grandfontaine honor them if he passed that way again, and take some hospitality at Morning River? Yes, he believed so. Soon, he hoped.

Elzada and 'Lon returned to the sloop. They wanted to be sure it would ride safely up and down with the tide, and wouldn't be in the way of other vessels. And, they needed a few supplies. The men were still at the shears, lowering barrels, and Elzada asked them if there might be a need for buckets. She pointed at 'Lon's buckets lashed to the sloop's deck. So 'Lon got rid of his buckets, but took in trade the groceries they needed. It bothered him. "It's not the same," he said. "Now and then I'd buy a bucket, somewhere up and down the coast, and once in a while I'd have to pay for it. Mostly traded. Then, other times, I'd have buckets I'd bought, or got on consignment, and I'd work them off and make a penny. But these buckets were mine. I made them. I pushed the damned plane and yanked the damned saw, and fitted—and made the beckets! First time I ever trafficked in something I had my heart in. Like selling your own flesh and blood!"

"Did you make on them?"

"I don't think I lost. They said they'd give me ten pistoles, and then they took ten pistoles for the stuff we got to eat. I don't know what a pistole's worth. I don't even know if there's such a coin! Used to be, but it was Spanish, I think. Maybe I just broke even."

They got into some clean clothes and walked back up the wharf to the governor's house. But they had no finery to match that displayed by Governor Grandfontaine when he greeted them at the door. His uniform dazzled. He was certainly all out to represent His Most Christian Majesty among the savages. He did the leg bit and kissed Elzada's hand. But the Indian woman didn't appear during dinner—the meal was served by a uniformed young soldier whose punctiliousness must have pleased the governor, but kept 'Lon and Elzada ill at ease.

There was still light enough after dinner so 'Lon moved the sloop to an anchorage. The heavy flavor of curing codfish persisted and was difficult to ignore. They talked a while about the dinner with the governor. "I'm turning in," said 'Lon at last. "Been a long day. Why don't we look around tomorrow and find out which way the Magdalens are?"

15

A call is paid on a Welshman at Peggy's Cove, but
he is no longer there to be called on

"You've been to the Magdalens," said Elzada, and
inflected like a question.

"Sure—many times. I get the idea you're expecting
some kind of enchanted island, like your Norumbega,
and I hope you won't be too disappointed. Lot of rocks,
not many trees, and fish, fish, fish. And stinking birds."

"There's a book home that tells how Jacques Cartier
found the place. Do you know how the islands got their
name?"

"Let me guess . . . I bet Jacques Cartier named them!"

"Wrong. That's one thing he didn't do. Long after
Cartier somebody set up a business there, and his wife's

name was Madeleine. So he named the islands for his wife. *Les Iles de la Madeleine*. Kind of interesting that she had sixteen children."

"I should think sixteen children would make it interesting for just about anybody. Got any idea why she tapered off?"

"No—but that's not it. Thing is, there are sixteen islands."

"Right on the button!"

"Cartier liked the Magdalens. He tells about the birds, and strawberries, and roses—said one acre of the islands is worth all of Newfoundland put together."

"One acre of anything is worth all of Newfoundland put together. I still think you'll find the Magdalens bare and lonesome."

But there was nothing dreary about the coast they sailed along now. When they left Port Royal a few fishing boats set out with them, but the fleeter sloop soon left them behind. The Fundy swells continued, pausing at slack tide to return again, but they'd left the worst of that astern. They didn't hurry. For several days Cap'n 'Lon held southerly, and kept saying he was amazed that the fog held off. That was fog country. When he left Fundy Bay and found his course northeast by a little east, he told Elzada some good yarns about fog-bound and stormtossed Cape Sable. "That's sand," she said. "Sable means sand. This is all French country. The English tried to call it Nova Scotia, but every time they sent somebody here to settle the French absorbed them, and Nova Scotia is still our plain old Acadia."

"There was one Welshman," said 'Lon. "I'm hoping we find him. Nobody yet has ever absorbed a Welshman. He had a log cabin on a crazy little cove, and there wasn't a tree in ten miles to make a cabin with. He towed every log to the spot. Don't suppose you ever ran into a Welshman? Not enough Frenchmen in the whole world to absorb a Welshman. If I can find his little cove it's a good place to spend the night. Nothing else like it I ever saw. Miles of rocks spewed around as if Godamighty had stirred all creation with an oar and laid it out to dry. This Welshman was crazy as a backhouse rat. Lived there all alone for years."

Elzada said, "My father used to have a little skiff built the same on both ends. He made it; called it his Welsh Canoe. He said a Welshman wouldn't know bow from stern."

"Not so. This Welshman was a good sailor. He had two sloops and a dory with sail. He fished and made his own cure and shipped dry cod to England. Had to be a good sailor. First time I saw him was at Arichat, on Madam Island. He said he'd like to have me stop in when I went by. So I found him, and after that spent many a night in his cove. We traded some, off and on, but that wasn't why he wanted me to stop. He wrote poems, and he wanted somebody to read his stuff to. I used to sit there on a rock and he'd read me his poetry. There's nothing quite like a good poem in Welsh."

And Cap'n 'Lon had no trouble finding the cove, which was even more so than he had described. Barren, wind-swept and seaswept, with great boulders and rounded ledges all about. A waste of desolate nothing, with this small and tranquil cove making in from the open sea. But there was no Welshman. Every vestige of him was gone—no trace of his cabin, his wharf, his fish house. Not a thing on the sandy beach to show anybody had ever been there. Cap'n 'Lon couldn't believe it. But he was just right about a place to pass the night—the water in the cove was placid and the sloop rode all night on a slack anchor line. Silence ended at dawn with the scream of a gull. They went ashore in the morning to wander amongst the rocks and boulders, and Elzada was amazed that God would leave such testimony to His carelessness. 'Lon said, "I never saw anything just like this anywhere else, and now that you've seen it—let's move along to something prettier."

And after some days of very pretty sailing along the Eastern Shore, 'Lon pointed and said, "That's the gut through there, and we could go that way. That's Madam Island on the right, and Arichat. But I'm going to hold off with this good wind, and we'll go out around. Everything you see from here on is an island. A big one." Elzada kept remarking on the lack of settlements—day after day of beautiful land and nobody living there. "Haven't seen a thing except that Indian village and Port Royal, and now Arichat."

"There's been places, but not many. We skipped some at Bay Fundy. All French. If we see anybody between here and the Magdalens they'll be on boats." He was right. From time to time a sail would be seen, and one afternoon they passed three boats together so everybody waved. The boats were handlining, so 'Lon sent down an offering of salt pork and soon had a haddock. Elzada took it below, but lacking milk she didn't go for a chowder but fixed fillets for broiling. She smiled while she was cutting the fish in memory of Marie-Paule's saying, "When you get the pan hot, catch your fish." This haddock would be fresh enough.

Then, still seeing no habitations, they came to Cape North, and 'Lon said, "All right—that's the end of the big island. Pretty soon now I'll throw the tiller and we'll be in the St. Lawrence River. Right now Newfoundland is dead ahead, too far to see. When I jibe, your

Magdalens will come dead ahead, about the same distance—Newfoundland and the Magdalens. We just keep
going all night, and we'll make landfall in daylight. If
the wind stays about the same all night, I'll shoot you
into Pleasant Bay about noon."

Elzada said, "Baie-de-Plaisance."

"That's it. But you get there through a dinky little
channel that's sometimes tricky. This sloop won't have
any trouble, but I used to be mighty careful with the
Madrigal. They don't have tide runs here the way we
do at home, so you can't always get off a mud bank by
waiting for a tide. We'll see, but if all goes well, tomorrow afternoon you can sit on Father Porkfat's doorstep."

Cap'n 'Lon trimmed sail while he still had daylight,
rigging the sloop so she'd sail herself for a few hours.
During the night Elzada was aware that he had stepped
out of bed, and she heard him going to the companion-
way. She called, "Anything I can do?"

She smiled in the dark and turned over to go back to
sleep when he said, "What—again!"

So Elzada had her first sight of *les Iles de la Madeleine*
in full daylight, exactly ahead as 'Lon had promised,
and they loomed with a fairyland loveliness that ful-
filled her expectations. But an hour or so later the illu-
sion vanished and, as 'Lon had said, there were rocks.
They still had a distance to sail before coming close.
Then they picked up Entry Island to their starboard
and passed Amherst Island to larboard. Next were the
"demoiselles," the two sentinel rocks that mark the
channel into Baie Plaisance. 'Lon used great care, and
had Elzada ready to handle sail if needed. And now
appeared Havre Aubert—ten or fifteen buildings, some
wharves, boats on mooring and some empty moorings

that meant boats at sea. And an acre or two of codfish
flakes with their far-reaching welcome. Nobody seemed
to be stirring in the village; nobody seemed to have
noticed the arriving sloop. 'Lon came in, headed for an
idle wharf. "Don't see Father Hermadore's boat," he
said. It would have been the biggest in the harbor, but
it wasn't there. Elzada pointed out the church—recognized by the three logs making a tripod steeple. She
could see the bell. "Thank you," she said. "I've always
wanted to see the Magdalens, and here I am!"

"Yes, and you've already seen about all there is to
see. Wait until the birds come home at sunset, and you'll
want far and away—hi-diddle-de-dee! First thing you
do here every morning is wash down the decks. Manny
used to say it wasn't the rocks—the birds dung the trees
to death." The sloop eased to the wharf, and a man
until now hidden behind a pile of gear looked up.

"Bonjour!" said Elzada.

The man approached. "Bless me!" he said. "Oi 'aven't
a notion! Oi knows what *bonjour* means, but not what
to do with one."

Elzada bade him good morning.

"That's better," he said. "Oi should know me French
by now—but Oi lets me French wife 'andle that. She's
the real Maudlin. Oi sye, you uses good h'English for a
French woman!"

"I'm not French."

"Then Oi thinks you uses good French for a h'English
lydy."

"Thank you, Would you tell us please where to find
Father Hermadore?"

"The priest—'im? Aye. 'Ees loikly sleeping one orff
in the front pew of 'is chapel, yonder. Bit of a tosspot,
'ee is. Not that I blyme 'im, being set h'orff as 'ee is in

this end of nowhere by 'imself amongst these 'eathen pirates. But still, 'ee mought keep 'is bad 'abits to 'imself, not to be public so much—h'its a disgryce to the bleddy cloth, it is. Father 'Ermadore, you mought sye, is h'indiscreet abaht 'is tipplin'."

"Sorry to hear that. Is he about?"

" 'Ees abaht. 'Ee was raht 'ere moments ago, showing a 'eavy list and ahskin' why he didn't see me in church Sunday. Me, in 'is church? Once, Oi was in 'is church an' 'ee was so raddled 'ee couldn't find 'is cup on 'is own h'altar. 'Ad to be shown the cup, 'ee did, by Pete Chabot, and 'im and Pete stood there 'aving themselves a tot like old topers, an' the rest of us sitting there dry as bones. Father 'Ermadore keeps a very low church. When Pete came down that Sunday, 'ee tripped and fell an' 'ee broke his thumb, 'ee did. You'll see Pete abaht, an' you can tell 'im by 'is crooked thumb."

'Lon said, "Don't you belong to Hermadore's parish?"

"Nah. Oi live on h'Entry h'Island. I just be here now mending gear. Me boat and two boys come for me later. Where did you sye you be from?"

'Lon winked at Elzada by way of telling her to handle that one, but she passed up the chance. "We're from The Maine."

"Don't know it, Oi think."

"Acadia—we're almost to the English, towards Boston."

"That's far!"

'Lon said, "Thousand miles or so—we came around instead of through the gut."

"Never been there."

When they found Father Hermadore he was by no means in his cups. He walked a perfectly straight line to welcome them. "Pax vobiscum!" he offered with the appropriate gesture, and Elzada bent one knee just slightly as she answered, "Et tu."

The Newfie chap on the wharf had overstated. At least Father Hermadore hadn't been tippling lately. But he had no aversion to a start, and he said to Elzada, "I have everything but your special touch—shall we celebrate your coming with flips?" He led them into his cabin, next to the chapel. It was neat and clean, sparingly furnished, and the windowless side was covered with shelves of books. By the fireplace at the far end was a table with a candle set in a wine bottle, and a chair made from a barrel—the seat thick with seal skins. Father Hermadore set out the other ingredients and then opened a trap in the floor and reached below to bring up a jug of milk, fairly cool from being below ground. He stirred some embers on his hearth and laid the poker in the coals. "You bring me happiness," he said. "You can see that my poverty is made worse by loneliness. The books" (he swept his hand toward the wall) "have been read many times." He rubbed his hands, watching Elzada compound the flips, and added, "I shall make a special Angelus this evening, and perhaps somebody will be curious and come—you can meet some of my Madelinots. They are all good people." He shrugged and smiled and said, "It isn't everywhere that the *contrebandiers* hear prayers said by one of their own."

Elzada passed him a flip, bowed with mock ceremony and said, "Pas de forbans?"

He shook his head. "No, mine is an honorable parish."

Elzada gave 'Lon his flip and explained: "A *contrebandier* is a smuggler. A *forban* is a pirate. The good Father makes a distinction. There are no pirates here." She lifted her own flip and offered a toast, "Aux Madelinots!"

Father Hermadore instantly raised his hand in a gesture of protest. "No, no! You will be here several days. There is no need to hurry. Let us instead, drink to a Madelinot. One at a time!"

16

The gannets, murres, and puffins of the Magdalens
signal Father Hermadore to the evening prayers

Father Hermadore excused himself and in spite of four
flips walked a straight line past his chapel to the house
beyond—a matter of some fifty yards. He had explained
that his housekeeper did not live in for two reasons. Her
husbands, who were the two reasons, were not often
home at the same time, but would be tonight, and Father
Hermadore hoped they might come for supper to meet
his guests. Carmelle, he said, had come from France to
be married to Pierre Bonenfant, a ceremony Father
Hermadore had celebrated at once. But during the winter Pierre had been lost at sea, and the next spring he
had married Carmelle to Joseph-Pierre Lebourdais. Then

Pierre, who had fallen overboard but had been picked up by a vessel bound for Marseilles, came home. The lamentable situation resolved itself when the three simply decided to live happily ever after. Carmelle returned with Father Hermadore. She was an outgoing woman, robust and hearty, of good shape and good face, and bouncy. When introduced, she quickly passed from Elzada to Cap'n 'Lon, and lingered until she found her French was lost on him. The kitchen was to the rear of Father Hermadore's cabin, one side of it given to his bed, and Carmelle now retired there to start supper.

"Jeez," said Cap'n 'Lon, "I thought she was coming aboard of me!"

Immediately the cabin was filled with a stinging, biting, blinding, choking wood smoke—Carmelle had kindled a fire and the chimney wasn't drawing. "It is always the same," said Father Hermadore, "she does everything in the grand manner! I can't convince her to start with a small fire. Always Carmelle!" It was soon after Carmelle made the smoke, and well before her husbands came, that the birds flew over. Cap'n 'Lon had mentioned the birds, and Elzada had read about them in the Jacques Cartier book. *Margaux, apponatz,* and *godez,* Cartier had called the birds, and he named one place *Rocher-aux-Margaux.* But these were not words that Jules and Marie-Paule Marcoux ever used—not that Elzada could remember. The book said the sailors took birds by striking at them with oars as they flew by. Now the birds came. A hum, a growing buzz, a rumble like thunder, and millions of birds flew over Havre Aubert toward their nighttime roosting rocks. Cap'n 'Lon watched Elzada during the passage and relished her expression of incredulity. The thunder of the beating wings diminished to a buzz, then to a hum, and silence returned. The flight was over. No, Father Hermadore had no English words for *margaux*, *apponatz*, and *godez*. "They will waken you in the morning," he said. "They pass to feed at sea, no one knows where, and then they come back. I ring my bell, too, but the birds are the signal for vespers."

Elzada went to the kitchen to help with supper, and she and Carmelle were soon chattering as women do in a kitchen. Father Hermadore excused himself and left 'Lon alone—he went to ring his little bell and to offer the evening prayers. He was back, 'Lon thought, with disrespectful speed. From the kitchen Elzada called to 'Lon, "Talk to him—Father Hermadore knows more English than he lets on. He'll understand you."

Cap'n 'Lon said, "Manny?"

Father Hermadore, having just retrieved his flip after returning from devotions, now set it down again, arose purposefully against all odds, and warily approached his bookshelves. He picked down a book, took from it a torn-out flyleaf, and brought it to 'Lon. "Manny," he said.

'Lon could read what was on the paper all right, but he wasn't sure what he was reading. He studied closely and saw:

Dom Affonso Manuel Henriques
Alferes Mor do Póvoa Varzim
entre Minho e Doura

So this was Manny after he went back to Portugal and claimed his inheritance! "Jesus to Jesus!" he said, and called, "Elzada!"

"My gawd," he said, "look at this! No wonder the joker can't write his own name!" Father Hermadore said

Manny was something like a baron—more than just a seigneur. Manny the Portygee? Son of a sidewinder! Probably want to be called His Grace! Manny? Be damned! Father Hermadore said as far as he knew Manny would be in England right now, and planned to come to the Madeleines. Then he would go to Morning River and Razor Island—and on to Boston to see that man with the face of the *boeuf-marin*. Neither Elzada nor 'Lon offered anything about James Mavryck. Let that ride for now.

While Father Hermadore was making a copy of Manny's fame and fortune for 'Lon, 'Lon walked down to the wharf to check the sloop and fetch a couple of bottles of claret. The Newfie was gone. 'Lon stood looking over the inland sea of the harbor and as he watched several small boats came through the channel from the ocean. Small sloops, and dories with sails—the fleet of Havre Aubert coming home for the night. 'Lon wondered if Pierre Bonenfant and Joseph-Pierre Lebourdais fished together from one boat, or from two. Musing, 'Lon surmised that a good and true fisherman might share his wife, but that he'd probably like to have his own boat. Something to think about, there. But as the craft approached, each had its single man, so Pierre and Joseph-Pierre fished alone! So much for voluptuous Carmelle, 'Lon thought. He took the bottles back to the cabin, accepting Father Hermadore's assurance that the sloop would be in nobody's way. Through Elzada, Father Hermadore explained that the men would salt the day's fish before coming along, so it would be a little time yet.

The cabin was smelling like a hot supper. The priest's kitchen fireplace had a fair-sized spit, and Carmelle had loaded it with ducks. Father Hermadore had said, "We never go without meat here, but as a consequence we

are obliged to like ducks." To which Carmelle added
that the next island over was a garden of herbs—the Ile
Brion that Jacques Cartier said was worth all of Newfoundland. There Carmelle would go to gather all manner of weeds and grasses that made the ducks taste
different from the herrings. She and Elzada would give
the spit a yank by turns, and baste the ducks from the
drip pan beneath. "This island here," Carmelle said, "is
only a *juchoir*—a hen roost—but we can live here so long
as Ile Brion is there." The gravy forming in the drip
pan gave her words meaning. It was agreed all should
have another flip. Carmelle said, "While waiting for
Pierre and Joe-Pierre."

Cap'n 'Lon raised his mug. "To Pete and Repeat!"

When voices were heard Carmelle went to the door
to intercept her husbands. They were carrying a piece
of net between them, filled with dulse. Dulse! Elzada
remembered how Jules and Marie-Paule loved their dried
dulse, and how they would lament that none grew at
Morning River. Whenever Jules went to the east'ard he
would bring back a bundle of dulse and try to get
Elzada—and everybody else—to like it. Pierre and
Joseph-Pierre were "enchanted," and Cap'n 'Lon winced
as he always did when he heard a Frenchman say he
was enchanted. Sounded lah-dee-dah. Something for kids
and gingerbread and fairyland. Enchanted! But Cap'n
'Lon shook hands and said, "Me, too—me, too!" and
kept his wince to himself. Pierre and Joseph-Pierre were
strapping men, not of a size to be led astray by elves in
the greenwood. Carmelle kissed both of them with wifely
vigor and handed them flips—which they didn't refuse.
Father Hermadore inquired if anybody could remember—did he go for vespers?

A supper like that, Cap'n 'Lon offered, was well worth

a trip to the Magdalens anytime. The ducks were just right. Juicy. The herbs from Ile Brion had covered any gamey flavor and had given them a new character. The roasted potatoes and lightly steamed turnips were assisted by a vegetable that Elzada couldn't name, in either language. Carmelle couldn't name it either, but said it came from Ile Brion. It was made delicious by the butter, but the butter—Carmelle said—was not from the cow. It was made from the drippings when pigeon breasts were being dried for smoking. Tomorrow, she would show Elzada her pigeon butter in her root cellar—butter will spoil, but pigeon butter keeps better. It was dark when supper was finished except for a small glow from the embers on the hearth. Carmelle reached the candle into the embers and when the wick caught she set the candle on the table. Father Hermadore was in his barrel-chair, sound asleep. His great ivory crucifix had slid over to make a clunk, but he didn't hear it.

Pierre Bonenfant and Joseph-Pierre Lebourdais walked 'Lon and Elzada to their sloop while their wife put Father Hermadore to bed. In the chorus of bonsoirs at the wharf, Cap'n 'Lon was astounded to hear himself saying "Bonsoir." My gawd! He was talking French!

17

Cap'n 'Lon explains the big difference between
smuggling and playing the odds at international
trade

The departure from the islands of Madeleine was blessed
vigorously by Father Hermadore, who brandished his
ivory crucifix in solemn appeal for a fair wind and safe
arrival. Carmelle had brought bundle upon bundle of
dried herbs from Ile Brion and they lay about the cock-
pit in 'Lon's way as he made ready to sail. Pierre and
Joseph-Pierre had delayed their start on the day's fishing so they could offer farewell, and had brought a gift
of several sticks of smoked gaspereaux of their own cure.
'Lon thus learned that a gaspereau of the Madeleines is
an alewife of The Maine, and he wasn't all that fond of

them either way. Father Hermadore clearly had influence, because a light air gently moved the sloop through the channel into the sea and then freshened northwest to hike them along towards Canso Gut and back into the Atlantic Ocean. Elzada stowed the herbs and soon had them hanging in the cabin, giving it the air of an apothecary shop. Even the smoked gaspereau seemed to lose their tincture in the overpowering force. By times 'Lon guessed they were making ten knots, and well before evening he pointed at a thin line on the horizon. "That's where we'll spend tonight."

Cap'n 'Lon had been there before, but not to trade— far as he knew nobody lived there. As the sloop approached, the thin line became a streak of red soil, topped by the greenest of evergreen trees, and by the time the sloop reached the little harbor that 'Lon was hunting, a brilliant summer sunset was far outdoing the crimson of the tidal mud and shore. "The red island" was 'Lon's only name for the place. And while he was at the anchor forward a shoal of fish broke by the stern, splashing red water into a red sky. He said, "How about a mackerel for supper?"

There in the twilight, full of mackerel, Elzada said, "What do you make of this Manny-Mavryck-Hermadore thing?"

"Been wondering about that. Years ago, when I'd put in at the Magdalens, there was a lot of business. Not just fishing. Real cargo. Schooners. And from all over— not just French. I could get rid of about anything, and could pick up the same. Today the place is down to pretty much Carmelle and two Petes, and Father Hermadore fat and happy. Where is everybody? You made a farmer out of me and I lost touch. Things have changed. I think the cargo moves just the same, except not in and

out of Havre Aubert. Do you suppose Father Hermadore has some kind of a seal that he sticks on papers to
prove a ship touched at the Magdalens? Or any other
place, for that matter? I could see how an arrangement
like that could save our friend Manuel Henricks Hooraw
a lot of mileage and money. And how about Mavryck?"

"Father Hermadore says smugglers—no pirates. Is
Mavryck a smuggler?"

"Matter of meaning. Hermadore says not. I guess not.
Then again . . ."

"Again, what?"

"Well, sometimes you look a little smuggley to me,
but there's a difference. Mavryck is clean. He can't afford
to smuggle. He's too big and important. Townes Estate—
you—you're too big and important. The thing is that
when you get big and important the rules shift. Father
Hermadore might be a smuggler, but Townes Estate is
carefully engaging in the manipulations of international
trade. How does that sound?"

"Sounds as if you called me a smuggler."

"No, no! Mavryck said he planned to let Hermadore
be cat's-paw on some wine. If the thing comes off Mavryck is going to make sure Hermadore doesn't lose,
because he'll want to use him again. Hermadore knows
that, and expects to make out. But he's got a kedge down,
just in case. If things don't work out, then Hermadore
is a smuggler. Maybe I don't explain things the best
way, but Mavryck and Hermadore will play each other
like two fiddles."

"But that doesn't bring Manny in."

"It depends. I think maybe it does. If what we've
heard about Manny is so, he's in a new league. He's got
wine to sell and wants his pay in things for Portugal.

The English will take his wine, and the English have stuff for Portugal, but the English have some funny ideas about taxes. Ideas Hermadore and Mavryck and Manny think about all the time. Makes The Bagaduce come to mind. My gawd! 'Zadie, do you realize what the landing tax would be on eighty to a hundred hogsets of Portygee wine set off in Southampton?"

"Would clearing through The Bagaduce amount to that much?"

"Hell! The stuff doesn't need to come to The Bagaduce after the routine gets set up. Hermadore says it does, and I guess Mavryck goes along, and that's good enough for Manny. Very simple."

"Not really."

"Well, there are ways to make port taxes almost painless."

"But couldn't Manny and Mavryck get together? Why Hermadore?"

"Good point. But the thing makes sense. One thing is that Manny is now a landed duke, or whatever it is, and he's back on the old family land, and he's got class. Remember that Manny couldn't even write his own name when he was just Manny. He'll be having a clerk— probably a priest, a monk—doing his papers and he'll be careful about going into shady details. He can trust Father Hermadore from away back, all broken in, and he doesn't have to make any explanations. Then, too, Hermadore talks French, and so does Mavryck, and I think that's the story."

The sunset was fading. Cap'n 'Lon said, "I been wondering about that Grandfontaine. He wasn't at The Bagaduce for his health, and he said he might go back. I thought Father Hermadore knew too much about

Grandfontaine for just gossip—sounded as if he'd looked into things on purpose. And I thought Mavryck expected to find more at The Bagaduce than he did—he was puzzled about what Grandfontaine was doing there."

"What did Mavryck expect?"

"Well, a place to unload and load cargo. A wharf. Grandfontaine was at anchor—no wharf. No cargoes. First, I thought Manny was keeping Hermadore on just out of sentiment—old time's sake—but Manny's no fool. So Hermadore's important. And Mavryck thinks so, or he wouldn't have gone to look at The Bagaduce. And whatever is going on is big enough so they don't smuggle much these days at Havre Aubert."

"I guess I don't see what brought Mavryck—me— into this."

"Boats. You've got boats. I think Manny didn't see that at first—it was Mavryck's idea. I think Mavryck woke up one morning with a sea-glin in both eyes and a smile that took in the whole of Boston harbor. This whole Manny-Mavryck-Hermadore thing is a hell of a big coincidence. Mavryck never knew we knew Manny and the priest. But why The Bagaduce? Mavryck talks to Hermadore, and wants to see The Bagaduce. Hermadore didn't cheer when he heard Grandfontaine was there. And to you and me—The Bagaduce is close to home."

Elzada stood and began to unbutton her shirt, getting ready for bed. She paused at the third button down. "The Bagaduce!" she said. "The Bagaduce! The Pentagoët! The enchanted paradise! Isles of the Blessed! This other Eden—this precious stone set in a silver sea! This Norumbega! I'm going to bed."

Cap'n 'Lon checked the sloop before he went below for the night. He came down into the cabin and took a whiff. "Jeez!" he said, "doesn't this place stink! Puts me in mind of Carmelle!"

Elzada said, "Good! I'm glad! But meantime, can't you make do?"

18

Through the Canso Gut and a visit to ancient
Arichat, with more memories of Manny, and then
pleasantly home

Today—that is, the 1900s—the Canso Gut has been
bridged, with a long causeway connecting mainland
Nova Scotia with Gaelic Cape Breton Island. The gut,
or strait, when Cap'n 'Lon sailed through with his Elzada,
was unobstructed, and ran some fifteen miles from the
Northumberland Straits to the Atlantic Ocean. Width
of a mile, and deep water. The bridge today is at the
Cape Breton Island end, carrying both highway and
railroad. The causeway was made from granite blasted
from the sheer hillside of Nova Scotia, leaving a hide-
ous gash to remain forever as testimony of man's pas-

sion for desecrating his Earth. Ships pass the bridge to use Canso Gut just as Cap'n 'Lon's sloop went through then. The Province of Nova Scotia charges a toll on the bridge only to eastbound traffic, presuming if anybody goes across he will eventually come back. There is no other way. The toll is accordingly twice as much. On the Atlantic Ocean end of Canso Gut, Cape Canso stands sentinel and the ancient town of Canso is close by. Ancient, because nobody is quite sure just when Canso was first a rendezvous for down-east fisheries. Opposite Cape Canso is Madame Island, where the village of Arichat has long been an active seaport and at times not unlike Havre Aubert in the Magdalens as regards contraband. It was at Arichat that Cap'n 'Lon came to know Manny the Portygee. 'Lon was there with his schooner *Madrigal* and some port officers came to check his cargo. Manny was able to keep 'Lon's questionable goods from becoming evidence, so a lasting friendship and healthy business relationship resulted.

So as Cap'n 'Lon hoped, the good westerly breeze held, and the sloop danced through Canso Gut. He put in at Arichat, where he would anchor for the night, and as he was earlier than he expected he walked Elzada through the town. He saw some changes, and then he noticed the vessel that had brought Father Hermadore to Morning River—the one that had a good Madeleine master and a reliable Madeleine crew. The same vessel that had taken Father Hermadore to Boston to see James Mavryck, and then home again. Elzada spoke to the master. She didn't try to find out anything in particular, and learned she wouldn't anyway—the skipper was closemouthed and didn't rally at all when she said they'd been to Havre Aubert to visit the priest. 'Lon opined this reticence confirmed his suspicions, except he wasn't all that sure just what his suspicions were. He did point out to Elzada that the vessel was riding high, meaning her hold was likely empty.

After Arichat, the course to Morning River was straightaway, with a dogleg after clearing Cape Sable. Cap'n 'Lon kept well offshore, and told Elzada, "If you spy Monhegan, we've gone too far." They spent one night at sea, Elzada taking a trick on deck, and the next morning 'Lon moved inshore until Cadillac Mountain stood tall. That night was spent in a quiet cove, and early the next afternoon they were behind Outer Razor ledge, checking the packetbutt. The packetbutt was empty.

Then Cap'n 'Lon tacked to kill time, and when the tide was right he laid the sloop up the estuary and touched tenderly at the wharf. Norman had come from the boat shop and Elzada, forward, had thrown him a line. He made a hitch on a spile, and the trip to *les Iles de la Madeleine* was over.

Norman said, "Welcome home! See you got rid of the buckets!"

19

A very pretty young lady comes to live at Morning
River and Mavryck looks again at The Bagaduce

June is all right if you can't do better, but along The
Maine they do better. The rarest days are in October—
then, if ever, come perfect days. The air is clean and
bright after September haze, and you can stand on your
doorstep and see amber globs of spruce gum shining on
the trees on the hill a mile away. The sea, in October,
is bluest of blue, and the sky is equal to that. The breeze
keeps warm in memory of summer and gives no hint
that November will have frost around the edges. October brings the flights of sea birds along the shore, and
grouse to the orchard looking for a stray apple. The
asters and the goldenrod, believing themselves the flow-

ers of fall, are mocked by the fringed gentians, which break out a blue even bluer than the sea and sky. October is comfortable, so the kitchen door can stand open without cooling the house. The bedroom window can stay up on its stick all night so—as Elzada was now proving—a person can step from bed all bare-arsed and stand before it to stretch and breathe deep without a shiver, without a goosebump. Cap'n 'Lon, sitting on the edge of the bed to pull on his boots, was grateful for a comely wife to stand between him and the window to adorn the sunrise, and was about to tell her he approved when she said, "Here comes Mavryck!"

One boot on and one boot off, 'Lon hobbled to the window, and there was the Townes Estate ketch coming up the estuary, her sails crimson in the dawn light but limp for want of wind. Riding the tide, she touched the wharf. It was too early for Norman to be at the boat shop, so a sailor jumped to the wharf and made a line around a spile. From the bedroom window 'Lon and Elzada could see Mavryck standing ready to step to the wharf, beside him chests and bags to come ashore. That something was afoot was easy to figure, all the more evident when Mavryck started up the path to the big house at a good clip. 'Lon looked Elzada over, wagged his head, and went down to the kitchen to greet the ugliest man in America. As Elzada dressed, she could hear the two men talking in the kitchen, but not enough to know what they were saying.

Mavryck was saying that this trip was not just for his health and a boat ride. Two-three things needed attention, and first of all—where's Elzada?

Cap'n 'Lon struck a pose affecting outraged offense, and said, "You got a nerve ramming in here before I've had my breakfast, trying to talk business before my wife gets her pants on!"

"Pants?"

"Yes, pants. She wears them in this house!"

But when Elzada appeared, she was wearing a dress, so Mavryck made his cumbersome smile that dislodged both ears and left his jaw under one of them. "No apologies for being so early," he said. "The tide didn't serve and the wind died, and we spent the night fifty yards away."

"You brought us a lovely morning!"

"And that's not all I brought. First things first. I brought you a housekeeper."

"A housekeeper?"

"That's right. I got the idea when I was here last spring. Here you are on the tag end of nowhere, and you and Nora do all the housework. Why should the owner of Townes Estate, I asked myself, be put to filling her own woodbox?"

Cap'n 'Lon handled that one. "The hell she does," he said. "If the boys forget it, that's my job."

"Not the point. If you people were living in the Townes house in Salem, you'd have cooks and maids and garden weeders and somebody to hold the door when you go out. There's people up to Boston can't touch a shilling to your million and they have people drive their horses for them. So, I decided Elzada and Nora could use some help. And for a starter, I've brought a housekeeper. She's on the ketch."

Elzada said, "I can't remember that I've made a decision since you came into my life. Do I get a chance to say no to a housekeeper?"

"Probably not, but try . . ."

"Well, I'm not sure I want to try. Kind of takes me by surprise. But I don't know as I need a housekeeper. I like my style here. I like to cook and sew, and Nora and I get along just fine. It likely isn't every woman would want to be stuck at Morning River; she'd have to like it the way Nora and I do. What makes you think this housekeeper of yours will want to stay here?"

Mavryck held up a finger. "She doesn't have a choice. Wait, I'll fetch her."

'Lon and Elzada walked down to the wharf with Mavryck, and one of the crew members handed the "housekeeper" over the rail to the wharf. Cap'n 'Lon said, "Well, Jesus to Jesus!"

The housekeeper was a girl that Elzada judged to be all of sixteen. Her lithe, but rounded, body was shaped to a dream, and her face was beautiful. She looked frightened out of her wits—her brown eyes had no more expression than a June fogbank. Elzada looked at Mavryck, and his expression was equally blank, but not from fright. Elzada turned back to take the girl's hands, as if to assure her, to comfort her, and she said, "Welcome!"

Mavryck said, "Elle ne parle pas anglais."

The girl was a deep, soft, chocolate brown.

Elzada had a flashback to the blackamoor who used to come on a coasting schooner during her girlhood, the only other Negro Morning River had seen. She thought how he used to roll a barrel of molasses, or rum, into the cellar on a plank, kicking it with his boot to steer it, and how nobody else ever dared to try that. And how he sang the old songs with Marie-Paule Marcoux while Jules played his violin. Elzada used to perch on his knee while he sang, and he would rap her wrist with his great black finger to keep time.

The tableau on the wharf, Elzada holding the girl's hands and comforting her, gave Mavryck his answer, and he said, "She's all yours. Cap'n Palmer had your *Blossom* at Saint Martin for molasses and he picked her up as part of the trade. Cost him five pounds. He said he could have done better, but one look at her and he got carried away. Funny thinking of old Palmer with a thin skin. But minute I saw her, I knew what he meant. So I let him charge her off at five pounds, and she's yours—lock, stock, and barrel."

Elzada realized well enough what was meant, but she said, "Five pounds? She's a slave?"

"That's right. But you can sign her off any time you want to—if you want to. Give her some writing. And meantime, she's on the payroll as your housekeeper and we'll build her up a nest egg.

"How come the French?"

"French Saint Martin. Cap'n Palmer couldn't find out much. She's some Indian. The Spaniards dumped Indians in the Loowards, her people among them. Somebody got fouled up with something out of the Congo, and here she is. Pretty as they come. What's the verdict?"

"I'm going to have the prettiest housekeeper on The Maine!"

"You can take in more territory than that. Now, she's intelligent, and Cap'n Palmer says she had good training at Saint Martin. I've got her fixed with clothes for now, and we'll see how things work out."

Elzada kept an arm around the girl on the way up to the house, and felt her stiff and strange. But halfway to the house that stiffness eased, and Elzada felt the girl snuggle. Her name was Barbe. Elzada coaxed her with small talk and made a special welcome as they stepped through the door into the kitchen and the house that would be her home. Cap'n 'Lon went to fetch the Kincaids, who knew Mavryck had come but were still at breakfast.

Mavryck said, "I found her French good enough."

"No trouble. Little accent I like. But she uses words that baffle me."

"She will. And don't forget you'll baffle her when you try to tell her about a snowshoe. Why don't you let her fry an egg and I'll eat breakfast?"

"A slave!" said Elzada. "I own a slave!"

"You can set her free. It's done all the time. Just like giving an apprentice some time, except you do it for life. Manumission, they call it, and we can record it at Boston."

When the Kincaids came with 'Lon, Nora and Norman had been alerted, but the two boys lost their manners at sight of Barbe. They just stared—stared at the first Negro of their lives. Nora took Barbe to her room— the one over the waterfalls, where the cascade gave the room its permanent lullaby. The boys carried things up and helped, still staring, to hang them in the wardrobe. Nora pointed, spoke an English word, and tried to get Barbe to say it in French. But Barbe got hung up on "bed," something she'd never seen. Then the forenoon was passed getting acquainted with Barbe, Mavryck and Elzada translating, and although Mavryck had some business in mind he didn't get a chance to bring it up.

When, the next day, Mavryck did get to business, he

had two requests. He wanted to go again to look at The Bagaduce, and he wanted to visit Monhegan Island. Cap'n 'Lon's sloop *Morning Star* was used and they made a family outing of the trip to Monhegan, Barbe included. 'Lon, Norman, and Mavryck visited the island men, and Mavryck asked a lot of questions—getting some answers. He said the trip was well worth while. There wasn't time on a day trip to climb to the top of Monhegan, so the others combed the shore. Elzada and Nora could see that the boys and Barbe would make out. No more staring.

Only the men made the trip to The Bagaduce. Since they'd been there before, there were changes. Now there was a wharf, and some buildings. One building was large enough for a warehouse and truckhouse. But no fort. Mavryck said he expected to find changes, and understood there was a fort. But no fort, as such, could be made out. Behind the buildings, towards the woods, some tepees stood—a dozen or so. Hard to count, the way the poles blended with the trees. "No need to go closer," said Mavryck. "I've seen enough. Turn home!"

"Now wait just a damn minute," said Cap'n 'Lon. "This is my boat, and just for the principle of the thing I'm giving the orders. I'll turn home when I'm a mind to, and don't you forget it!"

"Excuse me all over!" said Mavryck. "Bad habit I have. My compliments, sir, to the captain, and please to inform him he's free to turn home when he's a mind to."

"That's better. I'll brook no sass aboard the *Morning Star*. All my life I dreaded a mutiny, and I never had one. Always wondered what I'd do with a mutiny. I expect I'd be some tough. God forbid I'd have you ever in irons!"

Mavryck's jaw was now all a-wobble in his unbecoming version of mirth.

20

Now why do you suppose that Mavryck would want
Cap'n 'Lon to make a whole lot of barrels?

Nora had a lot to do with getting Barbe settled in—in
no time she had Barbe saying *fire*, *fireplace*, *fry*, *egg*, and
Nora was getting French words right back. Mavryck
was ready to go to Boston. He'd given the boys on the
ketch six days, thinking that was time enough to see if
Barbe would work out, and the ketch was due the next
morning. Mavryck came to the boat shop the middle of
the forenoon to say, "You got a bucket here will hold
together if I use it?"

Norman and 'Lon had been puttering, and just by
chance, not five minutes earlier, Norman had said they
ought to get rid of another parcel of buckets. The batch

'Lon had traded off at Port Royal had helped, but 'Lon kept making more and the pile in the boat shop proved the folly of keeping an excess of supply over demand in inventory. So Norman said to Mavryck, "Buckets he's got."

Cap'n 'Lon said, " What kind of a crack is that? Do you know anybody buckets a better bucket than I bucket? Guaranteed not to break, buck, buckle, or bend. How many you want?"

"Just asking," said Mavryck. "Thought if I could get a bucket stanch enough to stand the trip, I'd take some maple sugar and some smoked clams back to Boston."

Cap'n 'Lon spread his hands. "If that don't frost my arse! Biggest insult you can give is ask somebody to do something he's already done. I got maple sugar, clams, smoked alewives, eggs, some trout, some of Nora's molasses cookies, and one of my A-number-one buckets all ready for you. And don't bother to send the bucket back."

"Why don't you sell some of the buckets?"

'Lon looked at Norman. "You hear what the man said? Sell buckets? I keep making the things so Norman won't put me to work. I don't much like making buckets, but it's better than scraping a spar with a piece of glass. Only thing that keeps me sane is the pride I take in being the best bucket-builder in the business. Truth, now—did you ever see a better bucket?"

"Let's put all we can on the ketch tomorrow. Buckets sell. Make you a little money."

"Money, I need. Elzada has twenty-five buckets up attic full of money. Some night the timbers'll give way and we'll be killed in bed. I'll load the ketch, and why didn't you bring a bigger boat?"

"How about barrels?"

"No different except size. I make a barrel when we need one. But I don't get the knack of standing the things up to put the hoops on. Things collapse on me. Don't have the trouble with buckets and tubs. Matter of practice."

Mavryck asked, "Could you oblige me on an order for a hundred barrels? I'm serious."

'Lon turned to Norman. "We got oak enough?"

"Plenty of oak."

So 'Lon turned to Mavryck. "Why would you want a hundred barrels?"

Mavryck shrugged his shoulder. "Anyplace else in God's great world, you ask a man a question and you get an answer. But you tackle somebody from The Maine, and all you ever get is another question."

"So why do you want a hundred barrels?"

"To make Elzada some more money."

"Then why didn't you say so! We can always shore up the house timbers. What's another penny or two? Of course I can make a hundred barrels, but why can't you use a hundred buckets?"

"I can—I'll take all the buckets you want me to. But buckets are no good for wine. I want wine barrels."

"Wine barrels? How big?"

"Can you make them to size?"

"Any size. That cooper you sent showed us how to size barrels. Nothing to it once you know how. How big a barrel you want?"

"Pipes. Three tierces. That's about a hundred and twenty-five gallons, French measure. And they don't need to be set up. Leave them flat, and we'll put a cooper on them when we need them."

"I take it you got something in mind?"

"I always have something in mind."

"You want these pipes this week, or can I take my time?"

"How about next April when I come on my trout hunt?"

Norman said, "I can help with them."

"Good! And if you make two hundred, no harm done. I guarantee you'll get your money!"

Cap'n 'Lon said, "There you go again—money!"

Mavryck made one of his smiles, leaving the muscles of his face baffled, and said, "Money is a word that should never be said in that tone of voice. Never be disrespect-ful of money. Always say money with a rising note, like a joyous bobolink rising from its downy nest—like so: 'Ah! Money-y-y-y-y!' "

Afterwards, as they walked up to the house, 'Lon asked Mavryck, "Just idle curiosity, Jim, but how does a batch of barrels fit in with whatever the hell is going on?"

"Oh?"

"Yes, oh. There's Father Hermadore, and now Manny comes back to life, and Grandfontaine comes looking for Marcoux, and we make two trips to The Bagaduce, and you talk wine, and now wine barrels. Right?"

"Right enough. Townes Estate is handling wines. Good business. But in the past few years the business has muddied, and I've been looking around. Competi-tion and shenanigans. No knowing how things will work out, but I want to be ready and I think a few spare barrels might help. I don't mean to keep things from you, but right now that's about all I can guess at. But— if you hear rumbles from The Bagaduce, don't be sur-prised."

They had stopped walking, to stand while Mavryck finished, and now Elzada called to them from the door. "Come see if I've taught Barbe to make a flip!"

21

Jean Vincent de Saint-Castain, newly arrived at
Pentagoët, finds English squatters on his property at
Morning River

Cap'n 'Lon still had plenty of buckets left over after he
had piled as many as he could on the Townes Estate
ketch to go to Boston with Mavryck. And it was good
he did. 'Lon had moved his buckets outside the boat
shop to make room for his barrel project, and they were
stacked ten to a pile by the door. And there they were
the morning that the boat shop caught fire.

Fortunate there was no wind. Norman had the forge heating, meaning to hammer out some mast rings. The black smudge from the Tynecoal didn't dissipate, since there was no wind, and hung over the Morning River estuary until Nora came out and took down her washing. Forge smoke is a smudger. Cap'n 'Lon was sweeping up shavings and had a big pile right in the doorway. He looked up to see five Indians standing not ten feet from the platform, looking attentively at 'Lon as he swept. They looked as if they'd been standing there quite some time in silence waiting to be discovered. 'Lon let go with the traditional Morning River exclamation, standard since the days of Elzada's mother Martha. "Jesus to Jesus!"

This exclamation aroused Norman's curiosity, and he came to the door with a piece of red-hot iron in his tongs to see what caused it. When he saw the five Indians he forgot himself and dropped the iron.

No wonder. In all the years since Jabez Knight first came to Morning River, there had been but one other Indian to step foot on the place. That was Naddah the Micmac, who walked out of the woods on Elzada's third birthday to scare the hell out of Martha. Martha had watched an Indian at Sebago Lake sink a scalping hatchet into her first husband's skull, and it was a hard thing to forget. Martha had screamed, and afterwards Naddah became a good friend. But until now, other than Naddah, no Indians. Not realizing he had let the hot iron fall out of the tongs, Norman was giving his attention to the Indians. They were Indians, all right, but wearing pants and jackets not all that different from what Norman and 'Lon had on. Each had a pouch over his shoulder. Each had a walking stick. And each was wearing a billycock kind of hat made of beaver skin, with a broad brim for shedding rain, and a single white gull's feather standing straight up. The five faces had no more expression than one of Cap'n 'Lon's buckets. The Indians stood shoulder to shoulder, passive and silent, as if lined up for inspection. If they had weapons, none was in sight. Arms folded, they didn't blink at 'Lon's remark.

Recovering, 'Lon said, "Welcome!"

To which one of the Indians said in perfect English, "I do not speak English."

When Norman yelled "Fire!" and began stomping around in the shavings, Cap'n 'Lon joined him, and as they stomped they could see it was no use. The shavings were too dry. The boat shop was doomed, probably the barn—what else?

Intelligent men do not always respond intelligently to the cry of fire. They have been known to run in circles. 'Lon and Norman stomped, but stomping was doing no good. One of the Indians broke the trance-like formation by shouting some brisk commands, and at once the fire was out. At the commands, the other four Indians had grabbed up Cap'n 'Lon's buckets, two to a man, and in a twinkling had river water on the flames. The fifth Indian, the one who had shouted, continued to give orders and acted as if the whole incident was a military training maneuver. When the fire was out, the five Indians lined up again as before and stood again as if waiting for something.

Norman raked the steaming shavings outside, but there was no more fire. Cap'n 'Lon again said "Welcome," with new meaning, and he added, ". . . and thanks!"

"No English."

Surmising French, 'Lon went for Elzada.

"My gawd," thought 'Lon as he listened. "What a great thing to be able to do!" Elzada, shaking hands in turn with the five, bade them welcome—which 'Lon could follow. Then, which he didn't follow, she offered hospitality. 'Lon said, "Tell them thanks for saving the shop!"

Then Cap'n 'Lon understood when he heard the name of Jules Marcoux. These Indians, as Grandfontaine had done before, thought Jules Marcoux was still around. Elzada spoke in French for some time and turned to Norman and 'Lon to say, "I was explaining about Jules." The Indian who had barked the commands was the one who talked French with Elzada, and now he nodded his head, and then shook it. He understood, and was disappointed Jules Marcoux wasn't around. The other four Indians said nothing.

Then 'Lon said to Elzada, "Jeez! 'Zadie—doesn't anybody realize what just happened? We damn nigh lost the boat shop and God knows what else, and you stand there talking about Jules Marcoux. Tell these gentlemen that the management wants to buy them a drink. Tell them to follow you to the tepee!"

Elzada held up her hand to the talking Indian, causing him to fall silent, and she said to 'Lon, "This man's no Indian. He's as French as Jules Marcoux ever was. I've already thanked him, and he wants to buy some buckets. He needs buckets."

"You tell him to take every bucket he can lug off. They're all his!"

"And he says no drinks for his friends, but he'll come

to the house for a small wine."

It seemed a little downright to walk up to the house and leave four Indians standing there. Making his gesture, 'Lon stepped over and shook hands with each in turn, saying, "Thank you!" Norman did the same, and while Norman went back to sweeping out more wet shavings, 'Lon followed Elzada and the Frenchman up to the house.

Frenchman? He looked just like the other four. Same clothes. Maybe not so brown; must have twitched his whiskers. Not too old—hard to tell in those clothes. None of them was over twenty, if that. Wouldn't put the Frenchman at more than twenty, anyway. Had to wonder about the way the fellow shouted out his commands. Like a grenadier sergeant. Bark, bark! How come? The Frenchman was bowing Elzada through her kitchen door, and now he waited for Cap'n 'Lon to come along. "S'il vous plaît!" he said.

You don't translate *flip* into French. You just say flip, but you give it a twitter that results in halfway between flip and fleep. 'Lon heard Elzada's switch to a French flip, and knew she was telling the Frenchman he should try one. And 'Lon understood that he was willing to. "Want to get eggs and milk?" she asked as she stirred the fire on the hearth.

By the time he was halfway through his flip, Elzada had the Frenchman's story. He was Jean Vincent de Saint-Castain, proprietor of Norumbega, owner of Pentagoët, seigneur of Bashaba, and son-in-law to Chief Madockawando of the Tarratines. He savored his flip and nodded approval. "And," he said, "I believe this is my land." He pointed downward with his other hand, being careful to keep his flip mug level.

Elzada assured him he was mistaken and turned to
'Lon to say, "He thinks he owns Morning River."

'Lon said, "Are you sure he doesn't understand any
English?"

"Positive—not a word."

"All right. Mavryck said a few things while he was
here, and he's expecting something or other from The
Bagaduce. I don't know what, but maybe your friend
does. Maybe Mavryck knew about your friend. How'd
they get here?"

Elzada spoke at length with Saint-Castain. She told
him about the king's deed, by way of Commandant de
la Tour, and he seemed to accept this. How did they
come? Overland. They were looking for the old Long
Trail, and must have moved too far towards the sun.
Elzada told him that Jules said the Long Trail ran well
to the north. Her French? She thanked Saint-Castain
for complimenting her French, and again explained about
Jules and Marie-Paule Marcoux. Jules, she tossed off
the name, was a friend of Claude de la Tour. Times
gone by.

Grandfontaine?

Castain waved his hand to dismiss Grandfontaine. A
mistake. Grandfontaine had no interest in Acadia. Less
in Quebec and Canada. He was sent to fortify Pentagoët, to hold the country against the English (pardon
me!), and he had done nothing. Offended the Indians
so they went to the forest. No trading post. No fisheries. Nothing. Grandfontaine had been removed; he was
no longer commandant at Port Royal. Had, indeed, been
removed without honor! Instead, François Perrot was
now in charge at Port Royal; quite a different man. He
had been at Quebec; a man of considerable ability,

although perhaps *retors*. Elzada had a little trouble with *retors* when she translated for 'Lon, and fell back on her father's much-loved "chicanery."

'Lon understood. "He's a smart-arse—tricky."

"I guess that's it."

Elzada said to Castain, "Will you do us the honor of taking supper?"

"We've had nothing today—yes, thank you. But we will eat outdoors. My friends will not come inside."

Castain bowed himself out and went to join his men, who were sitting on the ground by the waterfalls. In silence.

Barbe had been down with Nora, and Elzada had potatoes and venison in the big pot by the time she appeared to help with supper. Barbe was excited about the Indians. "I'm Indian!" she said. That's what Mavryck had said about her, but to look at Barbe it didn't show. What red skin might have come from Mayan origins didn't show through whatever had happened at Saint Martin. Elzada patted Barbe's shoulder affectionately, and suddenly realized she shouldn't have—it was too soon. Barbe still believed owners didn't do that to slaves. Mavryck had warned about that. Elzada wondered how long it would take to persuade Barbe to sit at the table with her owner?

Barbe had no hesitancy about feeding the Indians. She carried out the stew, the biscuits, and the hot tea. She made small talk with Castain, but the others said nothing to her. She told Castain bluntly that she was a slave. The Indians spent the night on the ground near the cascade and took breakfast in the morning. Saint-Castain stated his appreciation of hospitality, and once again Elzada thanked him for putting out the fire. Then the five of them walked into the woods, single file with Saint-Castain ahead.

Each carried two buckets.

22

Barbe warms herself at 'Lon's fire; Madame de Saint-Castain appears, and we meet her small son, who comes to stay a time

Minutes after Saint-Castain and his men had left, Nora came boiling into the kitchen at the big house. Elzada was coaching Barbe at the hearth, and 'Lon was mixing some water and meal into a bucket of scraps for the pigs. Nora was exercised. "Nobody told me about the Indians!" Nobody had told her about the fire, either, because Norman was so upset he figured the news should wait for composure in the morning. So the boat shop nearly burned and five Indians spent the night—and Nora and the boys missed all the fun. Norman couldn't very well mention the Indians without telling about the fire, and if it hadn't been for the Indians there wouldn't have been a fire to put out. Nora kept saying, "The boys would-a liked to look at the Indians!"

"Next time," said Cap'n 'Lon, "we'll put up a sign and blow a horn!"

That winter passed pleasantly, too, and was uneventful beyond the usual comforts and pastimes. 'Lon did a little every day on his barrels, but not to overdo, and since he didn't cooper them the stacked shook took far less space than buckets. Norman had promised a sloop by spring for a man named Bill Potter at Pemaquid, but he stopped working on it long enough to make a new logging sled. Then he had to wait for iron to finish the sled, so he finished the sloop. When a boat did bring the iron, the winter had broken up, snow was skimpy, and it was time to tap the maple trees. Nora and Elzada did their winter's usuals, and brought Barbe along in the household arts. One thing, they made three dresses all alike for the Wednesday evening family meetings, and Elzada had a bit of a problem explaining to Barbe that a slave could, at least at Morning River, wear a dress like that of her mistress. Then she had to explain that just because she wore the same dress, Nora wasn't a slave. But as Mavryck had said, Barbe was intelligent, and bit by bit she was coming to take her equal place in the household. It was on that first warm May morning that Barbe made her big splash as a full-fledged member of the Morning River family.

There's a morning like that every year, the false harbinger of reluctant spring that has never yet fooled the people along The Maine. Cap'n 'Lon had kicked off the sheet, the only covering on the bed, at daybreak, and realized this would be the day to tease everybody with thoughts of spring. The snow was gone from open places,

ice had left the river. The tapholes in the maples had
dried up. Trees were greening. There had been peepers
the night before, responding in chorus to the good news
brought by a breeze from Bermuda. There would be
north winds still, might even be snow, and it was foolish to suppose summer was come. But this one was going
to be a good day, so Cap'n 'Lon laid the sheet back over
the still-sleeping Elzada and got up. For a couple of
weeks, now, there had been no effort to keep a fire on
the hearth overnight, so his first chore was to kindle a
new one. He kneeled at the kitchen hearth, blew his
pinch of gunpowder into a flame, and watched as the
flame caught his cedar kindlings. Give it a minute, and
then lay on some wood. By the time Barbe and Elzada
appeared, the fire would be ready to make breakfast.
Cap'n 'Lon sat back on his heels until it was time to lay
on the wood.

Then the kitchen door from outside opened, and
somebody came rushing in. Back to, 'Lon couldn't see
who it was, but it was Barbe, and she came straight
across the kitchen floor to back up to 'Lon's little fire,
her hands on her knees and her face level with his.
"Bonjour!" she said.

Barbe didn't have any clothes on. She was dripping
wet. Her teeth were chattering like kernels of corn shaken
in a tin mug. "Bonjour!" she said again.

Before he fled, 'Lon was able to answer her, "Bonjour!" Elzada was asleep but she came bolt upright at
his "Jesus to Jesus, 'Zadie!" and was sitting on the edge
of the bed when he got to her. The sun, coming gener-
ously through the bedroom window, made Elzada all
pink in her skin, and added radiantly to her naked beauty.
'Lon said, "I'm surrounded with 'em!"

Barbe's situation was understandable. In warm weather the pool was for swimming. She had awakened to a warm day, and not knowing how May can lie at The Maine about warm days, she had come from her bedroom to jump into the pool. Instantly, she learned that summer had not arrived. Nobody had told her that the great swamp above, feeding water over the falls into her pool, was still frozen and anybody could walk across it without wetting his feet. Barbe knew she had made a mistake. Numb, she crawled from the frigid pool, and dying ten times on the way had gained the kitchen where Cap'n 'Lon was still kneeling by his fire on the hearth. The fire looked attractive. She had backed in, spoken to Cap'n 'Lon, and hoped he realized how glad she was to see a fire. She wondered why he stood up and ran. The heat felt good on her tail.

And now Elzada appeared, quite as undressed as Barbe, and began to tell her that nice people didn't run around without some clothes on. Then Elzada began to laugh, as if freezing to death was comical. And Cap'n 'Lon stayed by the stairway door saying "Jesus to Jesus" over and over again.

Elzada told 'Lon the girl was pagan pure and shame played no part. "Meant nothing at all to her," Elzada said, and besides, the poor girl was too cold to care anyway. 'Lon said he'd buy that, but it would be well to see that she didn't parade around in front of Norman and the boys. As for him, he said, he didn't mind looking at Barbe, but he thought it would be just as well if he didn't have to do it every morning before breakfast. "Bad enough on me when you and I get in the pool," he said. "Comme la main!" said Elzada. 'Lon asked, "How'd she take it when you stood bare-arsed telling her to put some clothes on?"

Elzada said, "She brought that up, and I told her that was different."

"Eyah," said 'Lon. "That's right—from where I stood, I could see that the difference was only skin deep."

It was that same magnificent May day, but along in the middle of the afternoon, that the wife of Jean Vincent de Saint-Castain came from the woods along the loop of Morning River to present herself at the big house. Elzada and Barbe were picking over a mess of fiddlehead greens for supper. It happens that we know something about Madame Castain. At about that time a foot messenger from Beaubassin, the Chignecto neck that connects New Brunswick to Nova Scotia, came to Pentagoët with a letter from Governor Perrot at Port Royal to Saint-Castain. After he returned to Beaubassin he wrote how he had found the fort at Pentagoët in poor shape, but good enough so Castain was using it for a home and office. Stating his errand to an Indian, the messenger was brought into the fort and to a room where Madame Castain greeted him in excellent French. Since she was not expecting him, the messenger assumed she was in everyday clothes—in the French style and well made. She wore an off-shoulder dress that accentuated without revealing an ample and pleasing bosom. She was beautiful. Her skin, for a savage, was fair, and her hair, neatly arranged, was brown rather than black. The messenger wrote that Madame Saint-Castain was more attractive than many of the French women at Beaubassin—perhaps a tactless thing for him to write, but he was a truthful man. He found it hard to believe that she was the daughter of Chief Madockawando. Her smile was gracious, her hand immediate, and her grasp was warm and firm. "You wish to see my husband?" she asked, and led the messenger along a corridor of the fortification to a study, or office. Here, Saint-Castain was seated at a desk, a Greek lexicon open before him, instructing his son, who sat on his knee. There were other books. Castain set the boy to the floor, stood, and welcomed the messenger. After reading the message, Castain tapped the paper against the back of his hand, looked thoughtfully for a moment out a loophole, and then wrote an answer rapidly. The messenger returned the answer to Port Royal. So it was this Madame Saint-Castain, now wearing the forest garb of her Tarratine family, who appeared at Elzada's door. With her was her son. He was Bernard Anselme, grandson of and presumably heir to the Baron de Saint-Castain in France. She had brought her son, she said, at the command of her husband, that he might be safe at Morning River during some anticipated unpleasantness at Pentagoët. Her voice betrayed no emotion as she spoke, but her words conveyed that trouble was afoot and the life of her son was important.

Madame Castain was, as the messenger from Beaubassin had noticed, lovely and beautiful. Her name was Mathilde; her father was the Bashaba of the Tarratines. Her father, she said, had many daughters, and her husband had married three of them. She, Mathilde, then Thérèse, and also Marie Pidikwamiska, who was still a child. Father Thury, the priest at Sainte Famille Parish at Pentagoët, refused to marry her husband to Thérèse and Marie, and he was quite right. As a Christian, her husband must demonstrate to the Indians that a man should cleave to one wife only. So he was married to Thérèse and Marie only in the Tarratine way, and he was very happy and so were his wives. Her two sisters, she said, had gone with their husband—her husband—into the forest to escape danger, and nobody was left at Pentagoët. The boy was better off here than on the trail. She would not return to Pentagoët until it was safe to do so. Her husband begged that there might be understanding.

Elzada asked Barbe to run and get Cap'n 'Lon.

When 'Lon heard the story he said, "Mavryck said we'd hear something out of The Bagaduce—and to let him know. Can you find out from her what's going on?"

Mathilde didn't know. It would be ships. The fort was of no use. There were no soldiers anyway.

It was the Dutch. There was rankling still about the Duke of York and his taking New Amsterdam, and while the government of The Netherlands made no formal claims, it offered no reprimands to Dutch adventurers and pirates who thought up their own schemes. The attack on Pentagoët by Dutch pirates was foreseen by Castain and he vacated the place. The Dutch pirates thus bravely attacked an undefended fort and brought off a great victory. Had they found Castain there, this small footnote to history would be much longer, and had they taken the boy Bernard Anselme, he would most certainly have been offered at a bouncing ransom as the heir to the considerable Saint-Castain domaine in France.

So Bernard Anselme de Saint-Castain came to live at Morning River and stayed just about a full year, given to Barbe as her charge. It turned out to be a happy relationship—after all, she was part Indian, just as he was. Mathilde stayed a little over a month, proving a companionable guest. There was little Indian stoicism the

morning a vessel came for her and she said goodbye to
Bernard Anselme. She wept. She would come to Morning River again, but not for many years, and not until
this story is told.

23

Manny the Portygee returns to The Maine and
everybody is glad to see he hasn't changed
very much

When Manny the Portygee did return to Outer Razor
Island and Morning River, he came on the same vessel
that 'Lon and Elzada had seen at Arichat on Madame
Island—the one Father Hermadore had used on his trip
to Boston. Cap'n 'Lon saw the schooner come into sight
from the east'ard and recognized her, saying, "This has
got to be Manny." And he noticed the schooner was not
riding high in the water now, but was low in the water
and logy from a full hold. Even with topsail forward,
she came about sluggishly when she approached
anchorage off the Morning River estuary. By that time,

Cap'n 'Lon was alongside with a skiff. He shipped his laboring oar and looked up to see Manny by the rail, grinning like a rising sun and looking just about as he had looked when 'Lon last saw him. What was it—ten-fifteen years? So Manny was back, this would have to be the answer to things in general—Father Hermadore, Mavryck, Castain, Grandfontaine, The Bagaduce, Boston, maybe Southampton, even the talk with the fishermen at Monhegan Island. "Toujours pareil," Father Hermadore had said to Elzada about Manny, and here he was to prove it! No change. The same tanned face with the same quizzical smile—as if a joke under consideration had not yet been understood. The same lithe frame, with strong arms and shoulders, and the same seaweed-brown hair, ringlets showing from under what Cap'n 'Lon would swear was the same black knitted cap. Manny was good-looking. Now he moved quickly and came over the side into 'Lon's skiff with a seaman's agility that didn't jar the boat. He balanced on the stern-sheets and spread his hands with a gesture of, "Well, here I am!"

Cap'n 'Lon said, "Welcome home!"

"All is well?"

"Never better. We knew you were coming."

"The priest?"

"The same."

"So you know."

"What he told us, we know. He says you're getting nothing but cream."

"Cream? Yes, I think so. My father and my grandfather were robbed. I have what was mine. But cream?" Manny called to a deckhand, who soon handed down two earthenware jugs, loops of cord through the handles, which Manny gently stowed between his feet. "I have something for your woman, but it can wait. This (he pointed to the jugs) is cream from Oporto, and will explain everything."

At the wharf, Manny met Norman and Nora and the boys, Barbe and Bernard Anselme—but after he had been well welcomed by Elzada. Somehow Manny didn't look to Elzada like the standard-bearer for the city of Varzim, et cetera and so forth, Dom Affonso.

24

Saint-Castain notices that his friend Wenamouet
cottons to Barbe, and Elzada and 'Lon have a talk
about Barbe

Bernard Anselme was a good boy, mannered, schooled
ahead of his years, and he made his own agreeable place
at Morning River. He began to pick up English and
communicated this to Barbe, who thus was gaining
English better than Nora was gaining French. Then
Elzada noticed Bernard was teaching Barbe some Tarratine. And after two months of being at Morning River,
Bernard was reunited with his father. It was a strange
meeting—Elzada thought it was so unemotional as to
be sterile. Saint-Castain came from the woods one afternoon, with Wenamouet, and while Wenamouet stood

apart Saint-Castain came to the door of the big house and called, "Allo!" Elzada and Nora were in the kitchen, and he came in at Elzada's bidding.

"My son?" he said.

"He's well. I'll call him." She stepped to the stairway door to call up to Barbe, "Bernard's father is here!"

Bernard walked into the kitchen, stood about a yard from his father, and bowed ceremoniously. Saint-Castain bowed back. Neither spoke. There was no expression on the face of either. After a pause Saint-Castain said something in Tarratine, to which the boy responded briefly. They bowed again. Saint-Castain certainly noticed that Elzada was wondering about the lack of warmth, because he turned to her and said, "You will pardon our savage formalities." And there was no warmth, no emotion, no hug. The boy told his father he was being well cared for, was happy. He said his mother left about a month ago, and Saint-Castain said he knew that and she was again at Pentagoët with him and her sisters. "For the moment," he said, "the danger has eased." `

This time, Elzada insisted that Saint-Castain and Wenamouet come into the house for supper. Castain objected, saying Wenamouet would be uncomfortable inside, but Elzada said, "Don't you recall that in Rome you fast on Saturdays? It is our custom here to sit inside at table."

"Touché—I will persuade him."

Everybody was there for supper, and Nora and the two boys got their chance to look at a real Indian. Manny's port wine made a sensation and he explained about it in his limited English. A red wine from his own domain (Elzada used *domaine* in translating to Saint-Castain) made *fort* with brandy. This was the very first—until now port wine had not come to America, and not much yet to France and England. Then Saint-Castain interrupted to say, "I know—I am the first buyer. You have ninety-five casks for me."

So there you have it.

There was a hitch about ninety-five casks. Manny said he had ninety-four casks. Saint-Castain said no, ninety-five. Elzada, translating, had to explain that there is really no number in French for ninety-five—or for ninety-four, either. French, she said, stops counting at sixty, so instead of seventy you say sixty-ten. Eighty is four-twenties. Ninety is four-twenties-ten. Ninety-five is four-twenties-fifteen.

'Lon said he had no reason to disbelieve that. It was about what he'd expect. But how many casks—ninety-five or ninety-four?

Manny said ninety-four.

Jean Vincent de Saint-Castain said ninety-five.

The difference evaporated when Manny explained that he had tapped one barrel during the voyage from Portugal, and the crew had reduced its contents until it was out of the manifest. Some of number ninety-five was on the table, right now. And at a nod from his father, Bernard Anselme refilled glasses, showing he had already been coached in the gentilities. This reduced number ninety-five even more.

Castain said he hadn't expected the wine to arrive so soon, but that everything was in readiness at Pentagoët to receive it, and he would be there before Manny arrived by ship. Had Manny been paid?

Yes, Manny had been paid. Credit in London for goods he would trade in Portugal. Everything was in order. Cap'n 'Lon interrupted. "So what about Father Hermadore and Wopple-jawed Mavryck?"

Manny sat grinning while Elzada translated for Saint-Castain. Manny said Castain wouldn't know about Hermadore, but that he would know about Mavryck. Castain nodded and said, "Yes. I am dealing with Townes Estate, which is your M. Mavryck. I am told he is French."

Elzada glanced at 'Lon and then at Norman. Smiles were smug at the uncovering of a great truth. She said, "We know M. Mavryck. He is an old friend. And we are familiar with Townes Estate. But M. Mavryck is not French; like me, he is English and bilingual. How will you deliver these wines to M. Mavryck—that is, to Townes Estate?"

"I won't. A ship will come for them at Pentagoët. The transaction is on honor. Pentagoët, you see, is French at times, and at other times it is not French. It is for me to decide." Then for the first time Castain showed some warmth towards his son and reached to tousle the boy's hair. The boy smiled, and Castain added, "And sometimes Tarratine."

Castain told Elzada that when tranquillity at Pentagoët was disturbed and the people withdrew into the forest, a small boy might be a hindrance on the trail, and until things calmed down sufficiently, he would like to have Bernard Anselme stay at Morning River. There would be recompense, of course. She assured him there was no need to think about that. The boy was a joy to have around, and helped ease the situation with Barbe. Gave Barbe some responsibility. She didn't pursue this too much before Barbe and Bernard, but got Castain alone for a moment after supper to explain. Then he asked her if she had noticed how Barbe and Wenamouet had eyed each other during supper. No, she hadn't. "But," he said, "I thought a woman would surely notice.

Wenamouet was not at all uncomfortable at table, and ate little because he kept his attention on the beautiful demoiselle. I am surprised you didn't see that."

Sitting at supper table could be endured, but Castain and Wenamouet would not accept the comfort of upstairs beds. They went outdoors for the night, and promised to appear for breakfast. Manny rowed himself out to his schooner. And, in bed, Elzada asked 'Lon if he'd noticed Wenamouet making eyes at Barbe.

"God, no! Jesus to Jesus! Of course not!"

Elzada said, "It may be a good thing. I haven't talked to you about it, but it bothers me. Barbe is all baited and set for a man—and it doesn't matter one bit to her who he is. Fact. It's her fetching up. Every girl slave is expected to turn out babies. It's her duty. She's old enough, and if she'd stayed at Saint Martin they'd have bred her by now."

"What the hell are you talking about?"

"About Barbe. You heard me. It's just the same when Norman takes a cow over to the bull at Pemaquid. They have a man that comes around and breeds the girls, but before he got to Barbe they sold her off and she came here."

"Who told you all this?"

"Barbe did. Lately, it's all she wants to talk about. She's ashamed because she isn't making me a baby. Don't worry—I've talked to her. But we don't see things the same way. Now Castain's got me worrying about Wenamouet—do you suppose they'll tangle while he's here?"

Neither spoke for a time, and both thought about things.

Then 'Lon said, "You know, 'Zadie—she's a very pretty girl and built for downwind sailing, and there wouldn't be any great punishment to tangling with her.

Do you want me to go see if she's in her bed?"

"No! I told her not to try anything until I told her to, and I think she'll mind me. Did you have some down-wind sailing in mind?"

"Maybe Norman should take her to Pemaquid. Why don't we sell chances on her and take her up and down the coast?"

"Stop that—it isn't funny."

"I don't know why it isn't. If we find somebody to fix her up, do we get a chance to stand around and watch?"

"It wouldn't faze her. She watched the man breed the girls back at Saint Martin. When she first began talking about this, I thought she was asking about the facts of life and I gave her the whole lecture my mother gave me. But that wasn't what she meant. She knew all about the facts—told me how the girls liked everything."

"Be damned! Well, it'd be a cussid-fool thing for a girl to do if she didn't like it. Puts me in mind of something. Do you want to go to sleep now, or what?"

Elzada said, "What?"

25

Some reminders of how things were in those days,
and a few explanatory remarks about the situation
at Pentagoët

The common crook, when hedged with importance,
becomes "cunning," and "shrewd," and "clever," and
"crafty," and even "subtle," and when Elzada translated
retors with her father's favorite "chicanery" she was just
right about Governor François Perrot. When Grandfontaine, who was perhaps no more than a hard-luck
artist, was unceremoniously relieved of his sinecure at
Port Royal, Perrot came down from Quebec to take his
place. Perrot was crafty, cunning, and so on. And so
was Governor Temple of Massachusetts. The two of
them embraced an opportunity and became prosperous

cheating each other. The times were propitious. King
Philip had been disposed of but his passing did not abate
the Indian hatred for the pious Puritans, so for some
time after 1676 the English settlements between Wells
and Pemaquid, along The Maine, continued to endure
raids customarily described as "barbarous and uncivil-
ized acts by ferocious savages." None of this intruded
on the remote and sweet serenity of Morning River Farm
except as a passing coastal vessel might stop by and tell
the news, or perhaps as information forwarded to the
packetbutt by Townes Estate. But things were up in
the heaval, and normal trade declined. The French in
Canada were still having trouble with the raiding Iroquois, with a similar effect on business. Then, France
and England—in the context of New France and New
England—were occupied and preoccupied with various
schemes and counterschemes, permitting little thought
to the colonies. Temple, as governor of the Bostons,
had fostered trade with de la Tour at Port Royal, and
continued to do so with Perrot. Temple and Perrot had
a good thing going. Of late, Temple's nephew and heir,
one Nelson, was helping his uncle, and he was also a
good hand at the shady game. So now and then Cap'n
'Lon would look off from Morning River and see passing vessels, indicating trade between Boston and Port
Royal when, because of the heavals that were up, there
wasn't supposed to be any. And, now that you notice
it, The Bagaduce—Pentagoët—was cozily situated just
about halfway in the fabled Norumbega that both France
and England looked upon as theirs.

When King James ceded Acadia to France, the king
of France considered it quite droll, since Acadia was his
anyway. But Temple took this as a personal affront and
went on claiming The Maine, including The Bagaduce,

as his. Several times he sent shooting-ships up to The Bagaduce to harass and reduce—frustrating when nobody was there. The place remained strategic if sometimes vacant. Perrot, meantime, realized that Pentagoët was his all the time, but was willing to leave possession and ownership academic so long as his indifference turned a profit. So Temple and Perrot were jointly annoyed when, suddenly, Jean Vincent de Saint-Castain showed up at Pentagoët, very much in possession. Fact was, if you could catch him at home, he lived there. With the Indians. He fixed up the oft-buffeted fort, repaired what was left of the buildings, built a wharf with warehouse, and indicated his intention to stay there. It was an intrusion that called for thought. Castain was not just another settler—a *colon*. He was the resident proprietor of a considerable grant of land—the very special Norumbega. It was not an ordinary grant, but a gift from a grateful king for services rendered and valor on the field. An estate whose owner was a somebody—son of a baron back in France. And then again, not just somebody from France, but a somebody amongst the savages with whom he lived. His wife a princess; he might become chief. Certainly someday his son would become chief, the Great Bashaba of the Tarratines, and might even be the Baron de Saint-Castain back under the Pyrenees with another whole damned *domaine*. Such things must be kept in mind. Sticky.

Prudently, Perrot kept his distance and bided, but Temple did send another of his bang-boats up to bother Castain, and Castain, also prudently, retired up the Penobscot in good season and remained aloof. The historians mention a couple of incidents.

First, the millstones. Castain had ordered a pair of millstones from Temple's nephew, Nelson, in Boston.

Boston was the place to get millstones, and there was nothing wrong with this transaction. But somehow the millstones kept on going and arrived at Port Royal instead of Pentagoët. Perrot, in manipulating this, let his purpose weaken his thinking, because while Castain wanted two millstones at Pentagoët, nobody at Port Royal happened to want two millstones. The whole happenstance was ridiculous. Perrot had supposed Castain would make a big howl over the theft of his millstones, and then Perrot would expose him in high places for trading with the English. But Castain didn't howl. He just wrote a personal letter to the governor at Quebec and sent it over the trail by Wenamouet. This led to words of wisdom from Quebec to Port Royal, and about a month later two millstones were found on the beach at Pentagoët after a very dark night.

Then, there were the fishing boats. Perrot decided to go after a penny in fish and bought two smacks. Nobody knows just how Saint-Castain got involved in this, but it turned out he put up the money for the boats. Perrot found out he was in debt to Castain, facing due date and no funds. In spite of Castain's equity in the boats, he prevailed on the French fishermen until they refused to work for Perrot. In an extremity, Perrot hired English hands, and they robbed him blind. It seems that Castain didn't noise it about that Perrot had been hiring dirty English to work for him—he just let it ride that the cunning Perrot had been outsmarted.

It was soon after that when Castain welcomed to his wharf at Pentagoët a schooner flying the new flag of Portuguese independence with a cargo of ninety-four casks of port wine which was to be transferred to the aforesaid knavish English and carried to Boston. That was the day Saint-Castain shifted emphasis, so to speak, from Pentagoët to The Bagaduce, which meant the Portuguese wines would arrive at Boston under favorable tariff ratings—an arrangement already in effect for some time under the management of Governor Temple, himself. The ninety-four casks of port wine were put ashore and rolled into the warehouse. And Dom Affonso Manuel Henriques and Jean Vincent de Saint-Castain were shaking hands and bidding each other adieu in the manner of two happy negotiants who do not speak each other's tongue when the chandlery ketch of Townes Estate skipped jauntily into the harbor and tied up at Manny's ladder. Up came James Mavryck, as if he'd been reamed by a bait-iron from below, more than resplendent in a Townes Estate house uniform that was well on the expensive side of anything ever authorized for Sir Francis Drake. Manny had never seen Mavryck, but had heard he was ugly and knew him at once. Castain had no idea. Mavryck was plainly in great consternation. He wrung Castain's hand with evident heartiness and spoke rapidly in French, which Manny didn't understand but to which Castain nodded several times.

When Mavryck and Castain finished talking, they shook hands again with an enthusiasm that made Manny think of the old Portuguese saying, "Steal together, friends forever." Manny could see that Mavryck's agitation had subsided, and whatever had been wrong was now all right. The news that Manny had discharged and that the ninety-four casks of port were in the Castain truckhouse was good news. Now, composed, Mavryck turned to Manny and reached to shake hands. Manny was unadorned in his faded seaman's clothes and knitted cap. To him, resplendent Mavryck bowed in dignity. "My apologies, Dom Captain Affonso Manuel—I know you from the saintly Father Hermadore and our good friends at Morning River. Are you agreeable if we sail for Morning River at once? We, both of us, need to be there."

Manny didn't understand Mavryck all the way, but as Father Hermadore had said about him, he could communicate, and he nodded. Before Mavryck had gone down the larboard ladder to the ketch, Manny had his crew making sail. Jean Vincent de Saint-Castain, in the midst of his family of Tarratines, stood on the wharf at Pentagoët and watched the two vessels out of sight—the ketch well ahead.

26

"L'affaire des vins, assez insignificante en somme,
allait avoir des conséquences d'une grande portée
pour Saint-Castain, et, en définitive, orienter sa vie."

Daviault

The chandlery ketch arrived at Morning River some-
time ahead of Manny's schooner. James Mavryck, no
longer in his jackanapes uniform, jumped to the wharf
and met Cap'n 'Lon about halfway from the boat shop.
He waved aside any greeting Cap'n 'Lon might have
offered and called, while they were still fifteen feet apart,
"How many barrels did I get in April?"

"All I had."

"Well—how many did you have?"

"Not's many as I thought."

"Well—God Almighty!"

"My sentiments. What are you all heifered up about? You come in here boiling and jump ashore swinging. This is Morning River! Simmer down!"

Mavryck took a deep breath and said, "All right. Forget it. Manny the Portygee's behind me, and when he gets here we'll talk. I've been heifered up for a week, and maybe a flip will settle me some. Need anything off the ketch?"

"Not for a flip, we don't."

By the time the ketch had retreated down the estuary to her anchorage, Manny's schooner had arrived and a seaman had rowed Manny ashore. Flips followed at the big house and an agreement prevailed that Elzada had well taught her nut-brown West Indian slave the gentle art of decanting a down-Maine flip. "I guess," said Mavryck, "that I'm not all that bad at picking housekeepers." Then, returning to the barrels, he learned from Elzada that the count last April had been fifty-six. Norman said he counted a few days ago, and Cap'n 'Lon had turned out sixty-four more since April. Cap'n 'Lon insisted he was never interested enough to keep track. "But I may have made two-three more since Norman looked."

"It's enough," said Mavryck, "we're all set," and then came the flip-punctuated wait until he should bring darkness from light and tell the rest.

"That port wine our friend Dom Affonso just left at The Bagaduce is yours," he told Elzada. "Bought and paid for by Townes Estate. Fair and square, money on the dot. Manny takes his pay in London. Castain in the middle. Now, just about daybreak tomorrow, our—your—topsail schooner *Vashti* will be at The Bagaduce to pick up ninety-four casks of port and run them into Salem. They'll come in under English registry, from New England territory. No questions asked, no favors granted. The wine will be disposed of variously, as we say, from time to time, and if you ever bother to look at your company reports you'll see that you paid a generous commission to Nelson, Watson, and Associates at The Bagaduce."

At this, Manny made a kind of a snort, a little more powerful than a chuckle, indicating that he was amused.

Mavryck said, "All right. Nelson is the bahstidly nephew of bahstidly Governor Temple, and he's no good either. We set him up for his name—there's no such outfit as Nelson, Watson, and Associates. Right now, closest to Nelson, Watson, and Associates is your French-Indian friend over at The Bagaduce. That's what Dom Manuel is laughing at."

"So, what's kept you all roiled up for the past week and brings you here all in a stew?"

Mavryck turned to look at 'Lon, and in so doing brought his flip mug to Barbe's attention. After Barbe topped it off, Mavryck followed her with his eyes to watch her do the same for Dom Affonso Manuel Henriques Alferes Mor do Póvoa Varzim entre Minho e Doura—that is, Manny the Portygee. Manny offered no remonstrance, and Mavryck noticed no reluctance by Barbe. Mavryck spoke. "We got word this Nelson and his damned uncle had plans to go after Manny's cargo of port. When I got to The Bagaduce I expected to find we'd been robbed. When Castain said the cargo was unloaded and safe in his warehouse, I didn't believe it. If the *Vashti* makes schedule and takes the wine tomorrow, that's that."

"All fussed up over nothing." Cap'n 'Lon reached his mug towards Barbe, but she was over by Manny and didn't notice.

"Barbe!" said Elzada.

"Thanks," said 'Lon.

"Fussed up, yes, but not over nothing," from Mavryck. "The minute I heard our wine was safe, I knew we'd made the wrong guess. It wasn't Manny's wine they were after. It's got to be another cargo of wine."

"Riddles, riddles," said Elzada.

Mavryck nodded. "Yes. This damned Temple has been a skunk in the buttery all along. He claims The Bagaduce is his—not England's, but his. He and Perrot down east aren't happy that Castain moved in and muddied the water. They're out to get him."

"Seems to me," said Elzada, "that you've—we've —been using The Bagaduce too. What's the difference?"

"Big difference. Castain owns the place. It's his. He's there with official standing. And what we do with Castain is aboveboard and lawful. All on honor."

"That's what he said when he was here—on honor."

"It is. He's honest goods. But he's sharp, and he doesn't like Perrot. That's what we heard, and I supposed they were going to strike at him through Manny, here."

"But they didn't—so we're safe home and no broken bones."

"I don't think so. Not yet. That's why I want 'Lon's barrels."

"You got more to tell us."

"I got more I'm just guessing at. Castain has another shipment of wine due—not ours, not Manny's—I figure it's going to be used as evidence against Castain. Temple and Perrot will use it to prove Castain is all cushy-cow-bonnie with the dirty English. Raise hell with him. Good, honest, upright Frenchman turned traitor."

Elzada protested at that. "No—you're talking both sides at once. Castain is trading with *us*."

"Same big difference. And I made the mistake thinking Temple and Perrot were after us—you—and I was wrong. Next time I'm going to be right."

"And when is next time?"

"Right away. Week or so." Mavryck turned to Manny, whose attention was on Barbe, so Mavryck had to say, "Manny!"

"Manny, will you take Cap'n 'Lon's barrel shook over to Pemaquid tomorrow morning? There's a cooper there, and he has the barrels I got last April. He'll set up the rest of them, and then you take the whole batch—going to be over a hundred—up to The Bagaduce and put them on the wharf. Our friend Castain, who can be trusted, knows they're coming and he knows what to do with them. He and I got together enough so he knows. Understand?"

"How long does this take?" asked Cap'n 'Lon.

"Two days. No more than three. The cooper's ready and waiting, and he has two helpers. After that, I'd like Manny to bring his schooner back here." Mavryck looked at Barbe. "If he doesn't mind."

Manny nodded. Possibly misjudging his nod, Barbe filled his mug. Manny nodded again. Cap'n 'Lon said, "He's got it—good as done."

Mavryck tilted back on his stool, looked into his flip mug, waggled his massive head, and broke out one of his devastating smiles. He said, "Who has more fun than I do?"

27

Mavryck and young Bernard Anselme de Saint-
Castain socialize, and the boy talks about Pentagoët

During the flip session, Bernard Anselme de Saint-Castain had been upstairs reading. When he came down to
supper, he and Mavryck hit it off like ancient buddies.
Mavryck was much taken with the boy. They talked
until bedtime, Mavryck doing most of the listening, and
Bernard told Mavryck a great deal about Indian life at
Pentagoët. Elzada was amused that Mavryck adroitly
drew the boy out about some things his father might
have preferred to leave less public. But, Mavryck did
have his way. . . . The boy was up at daylight the next
morning to help with loading the barrel shook on Manny's schooner, and as there was an early tide this was

done well before Elzada and Barbe had the oatcakes,
eggs, maple syrup, potatoes, and strips of bacon on the
table. Manny was well on his way to Pemaquid when
breakfast began at Morning River. Oh, yes—Mavryck
had asked Manny to stop at the ketch on his way by
and ask a hand to come ashore.

As Barbe started to clear away the breakfast dishes,
Elzada told Mavryck about her misgivings over the girl.
She said, "She's obsessed with the idea of having a baby
for me."

Mavryck said, "You got to admit she's equipped to
do that."

"You men! I get all of that stuff I need from 'Lon! I
don't want a slave baby, and I don't think you're funny.
When Castain was here, he noticed she was making up
to his friend. The friend didn't mind. Next day I gave
her what-for, and she promised me she'd keep her knees
together. But she's hotter than a wounded skunk, and I
do worry. Worry? Well, maybe she's safe from Norman, but what about my raunchy old captain, here?
And now Manny. You saw how she went for Manny!"

Cap'n 'Lon said, "Damned if this isn't interesting! Here
we sit talking about the girl, and she's hearing every
word we say. Her and the boy, too. Hears it all, and
hasn't the slightest. What was that you said about me?"

"You heard me, and you better damn-well heed. But
we can't talk in front of Barbe forever—she's picking up
English every day. Yesterday she banged her shin and
said 'Jesus-to-Jesus.' "

'Lon said, "You can't blame that on me."

Mavryck said, "The thing to do is get some good
Christian ideas into her head and break her away from
what she grew up with."

"Don't think I haven't tried. And I've made progress.

At least she doesn't run around in her skin any more. But a girl doesn't have to be a slave to want her tail explored. Difference is that Barbe thinks it's a duty. She owes me. Gave me goosebumps to realize she's ashamed *not* to be up a stump. So, what do you think?"

Thinking was interrupted by the arrival at the door of a young man from the ketch, asking for instructions. Cap'n 'Lon and Mavryck stepped outside to talk to him. Cap'n 'Lon explained to the lad just where a vessel coming down from Boston would turn to make up into Penobscot Bay and come to The Bagaduce. Then Mavryck told the boy to take the ketch there and wait to intercept a schooner. She would be, he felt sure, the *Jeannie* out of Piscataqua or Portsmouth, with a cargo of wine consigned to Nelson, Watson, and Associates at Pentagoët—The Bagaduce. The ketch was to sail back and forth until this schooner appeared, which might be a day or two, and even more. Then, with compliments from James Mavryck of Townes Estate, the master of the *Jeannie* was to be asked to change course and come to Morning River, where his servant, James Mavryck, would explain and give him further instructions. This is of gravest importance, and the master of *Jeannie* should be made aware that there is danger if he does not come to Morning River. Is that understood?

"Yes, sir—perfectly."

"All right. Then you are to ask the master the precise number of casks of wine he has for Nelson and Watson. Not a round number, but exact. Next, you go to Pentagoët—that's The Bagaduce—and you tell them there just what that exact number is. Write it down and show them, because they talk French and you don't. Understand?"

"Perfectly."

"Good. And that done, come back here."

"Yes, sir."

The lad walked down the path to return to the ketch, and Cap'n 'Lon and Mavryck went back into the house. Elzada was still at table, making small talk with Bernard Anselme, and Barbe was still at the dishes. "Now," said Mavryck, "what's all this about the young lady being in a family way?"

28

And now appears Captain Philip Syruet, who finds
Norumbega, in his turn, a beautiful place, but
doesn't reach The Bagaduce

On the tenth day of August, 1686, the schooner *Jeannie*,
laden with one hundred and two casks of Gironde wines,
stood out of Portsmouth on the Piscataqua and rode the
outgoing tide hell-bent for breakfast into the open sea.
Her master, Captain Philip Syruet, was following orders
but he wasn't sure just what was going on. He had taken
on his cargo in the usual way at Bassin Arcachon,
expecting as usual to make the usual voyage to Lübeck.
But at the last moment a vessel arriving from Boston
had spoken him, and a sealed packet brought him a
change in orders. Instead of Germany, he would take

his cargo to Boston. He had, but at Boston he was told to proceed to Portsmouth and wait for further orders. After he'd been some time at Portsmouth, orders came by overland post that he was to go down to The Maine and deliver his wines to Nelson, Watson, and Associates at The Bagaduce. By this time Captain Syruet was happy to do anything that would lighten his hold and let him get back to work, so he asked no questions except where the hell is The Bagaduce, anyway? Learning it was to the east'ard, beyond Monhegan, in Norumbega Bay, he embraced the voyage eagerly as he had never sailed those waters and had heard that The Maine is beautiful. He accordingly dallied, putting in at several places just to see what might be seen, and after some days came to Monhegan Island, which he admired and where he received hospitality. It was on the fifteenth of August that he stood out from Monhegan, setting a course just east of north—towards the distant hills— expecting to reach the fabled wonder city of Bashaba reasonably early in the afternoon. Captain Syruet was an able mariner and took great precautions when he approached the mainland and saw the churning craggy ledges that would be unkind to unwary ships with precious cargo. As the *Jeannie* rounded from the open sea into the great bay of Penobscot itself, the beauty of the land, with the blue hills, delighted him—as it delighted all before and has delighted all since—and he spoke to his mate to be sure and include all this lovely scenery in the log. It was about that moment that the masthead sang out that there was a sail dead ahead.

The Townes Estate chandlery ketch was a lovely little boat at sea. Built as a sloop, although longer than most sloops of her time, she had been given an after mast not just to increase her speed, but to give her more ease in moving about Boston harbor as she provisioned vessels. She had a crew of four, but in addition to sailing and tidying the ketch, the crew did the deckwork of loading and unloading groceries and gear. Then, too, the ketch was the welcome-boat of Townes Estate, a floating advertisement that goods and services were available. This called for a show of bunting, trim and neat appearance, snap and ginger from the crew, and distinctive—almost gaudy—uniforms. The ketch was one of a kind. Since Captain Syruet of the *Jeannie* had seen the ketch at Boston many times, he recognized her when she approached, and he was in no way suspicious when she spoke him and asked permission to come board. James Mavryck had foreseen that there would be curiosity as to why the Townes Estate ketch was at Norumbega, and felt intercepting the *Jeannie* would not be difficult. Captain Syruet luffed, told a hand to make a line from the ketch secure, and thus received the message that he was to pass directly to Morning River without touching in at The Bagaduce. He reasoned that Townes Estate would not be playing games, and besides—this voyage had been an odd one from the start, anyway. The ketch then set out for The Bagaduce with the magic number "102" while Captain Syruet turned easterly towards Morning River. As he brought his *Jeannie* into quiet water behind the Razor islands, James Mavryck was waiting in a skiff to greet him—Cap'n 'Lon at the oars.

"French or English?" called Mavryck.

"Either one."

"English, then. Welcome to The Maine! Mavryck here. May I come aboard?"

By the time the *Jeannie* was anchored and things secured for the night, the Townes Estate ketch came skipping by to signal that "102" had been delivered.

Captain Syruet followed James Mavryck down the *Jeannie*'s ladder, and Cap'n 'Lon rowed the skiff up to the wharf. The usual flip hour made Captain Syruet feel most welcome indeed, and as the waning day drew upon the supper hour he was increasingly aware that Madame Plaice was a charming and agreeable woman, that Mademoiselle Barbe was sweet and pretty and friendly, and that flip was an acknowledged cure for what ailed you. Barbe was excited to find Captain Syruet spoke French, but contrived to fill his mug each time so he didn't have to ask.

29

In consequence of this and that, a considerable group
accumulates at Morning River both afloat and ashore

Captain Philip Syruet was understandably impatient at
being kept at anchor with his full hold, but James Mavryck kept assuring him the delay would prove well worth
while. When Elder Brewster was first at Plymouth,
Massachusetts, he was told, "If you ever want anything
done right away, never go to Pemaquid." Accordingly,
four days went by before the cooper at Pemaquid had
finished setting up Cap'n 'Lon's barrels, and then it took
a day to run the barrels up to The Bagaduce aboard
Manny's schooner. For which time Cap'n Syruet bided
at Morning River. The actual count on Cap'n 'Lon's
barrels as Manny left Pemaquid with them was one

hundred and twenty-three. He must have made a few that got skipped in the count. The magic number of one hundred and two was tallied at the wharf at The Bagaduce, and Manny and Saint-Castain counted them again to be sure. They stood row on row as Manny up-sailed and headed for Morning River. Manny had most of the over-count in his hold, but a few on deck, and as the weather promised to be comfortable he didn't lash them. Castain and his wives had asked Manny to take supper, but he was shy because of a language shortage, and he went aboard of his boat to pass the night with his Portuguese and Madeleines crew. He got away early next morning, and was at Morning River with his anchor down well before noon.

James Mavryck had 'Lon row him down in a skiff at once, and Manny assured him exactly one hundred and two empty barrels were arrayed in plain sight on the wharf at The Bagaduce. So Mavryck had 'Lon set him over to the *Jeannie* where he told Captain Syruet all was well. "We cut it close," he said, "but I figure two days and you can sail."

Up at the big house, afterwards, Elzada said, "Never had this many people at Morning River before. More'n enough for a clambake!"

Mavryck said, "I give you fair odds there'll be more. I expect Saint-Castain to show up anytime—he'll come now to get his boy."

And as usual, Mavryck was right. Castain and Wenamouet walked out of the woods the next afternoon. They were in trail garb, with pouches and blankets.

30

Captain Thomas Sharpe, in his turn, visits Bashaba
and, in turn, finds nobody there, but the region is
beautiful

The records don't tell us if Judge Nathaniel Palmer of
Pemaquid was in cahoots with Governors Temple and
Perrot as they conspired to steal the wines of Pentagoët
and discredit Jean Vincent de Saint-Castain. One may
fairly guess he was not, because it wasn't necessary. At
this late date, anyway, we can give him the benefit of
the doubt. He was probably no more than a willing cat's-
paw. Even so, one should never assess the sycophants
and disciples of Lady Law in terms used for honest and
respectable people. The judicial mind is never con-
cerned with right and wrong. Let it be unjust and

immoral, but if it is "lawful" the judge and the lawyer will embrace the unjust and the immoral. So let us presume Judge Palmer rendered his decision on the law as he desired it and on the evidence as he heard it, allowing for the fact that the plaintiff was governor, and agent, lawfully, for the Duke of York. We have no information to make us think Judge Palmer would have ruled against his own best interests.

The evidence was certainly sufficient, and nothing contradicted it. If the governor, himself, made the accusations, that should suffice. The solid information at hand indicated that a shipload of French wines was on its way to be unloaded at The Bagaduce—English territory. The vessel was *La Jeanne*, but in keeping with the present deceit she was now *Jeannie*, and although she had a French cargo and a French master, she purported to be out of the Piscataqua. The inference, noted by Judge Palmer, was clear—after discharge the wines would be reshipped for sale in, say, Boston, contrary to statutes made and provided, and with intent to evade duties. Appended were papers touching on discovery, possession, occupation, treaty, and common sense proving The Bagaduce was English. Furthermore, the wines were consigned to Nelson, Watson, and Associates—a fictitious firm existing only to lend respectability to fraudulent and illicit transactions. Jean Vincent de Saint-Castain was guilty of numerous unlawful acts, as stated. The wines, once landed at The Bagaduce, were contraband, forfeit, and should be confiscated. Jean Vincent de Saint-Castain should be arrested, charged with evasion, conspiracy, and willful violation of English law, to stand trial before said court of said jurisdiction, &c.

That's the way Judge Palmer saw it. He ordered relief

to the much-abused Governor Temple. And he directed
Captain Thomas Sharpe, who happened to be at Pemaquid at that very moment with his gunboat and marines,
to proceed at once to The Bagaduce, to seize the vessel
La Jeanne and its contraband cargo, to arrest its Captain
Syruet and said Saint-Castain, and bring all to justice.
Which came to pass, but not quite. Captain Sharpe
arrived at The Bagaduce, men and guns at the ready,
and was puzzled at what he found. Captain Syruet and
La Jeanne had come and gone, but the cargo of wines
was arranged, cask by cask, on the wharf in orderly
fashion as if ready to be loaded for reshipment. There
was nobody about. The warehouse showed signs of
recent activity, but it stood empty. The fort, not in good
condition, seemed to be used as a home, but it was not
furnished too comfortably and the only real evidence of
recent use was an open book on a table. Other buildings
were sparsely furnished and were either used or unused—
it was hard to tell. Back from the water, by the woods,
stood some wigwams, but they were empty. One of the
marines tinkled Father Thury's bell, and it rang plain-
tively across the clearing to cause the other marines to
look up. One hundred and two casks. They were contraband, and after Captain Sharpe unlimbered a derrick, they were confiscated.

Captain Sharpe saw no reason to be severe beyond
taking the wines, so he left Pentagoët as he found it—
except for a hundred and two casks of Gironde wines
in his hold. They would be assigned to the court as
evidence of assorted crimes pending against Jean Vincent de Saint-Castain, enemy of the crown. Captain
Sharpe was unhappy that he had come too late to appre-
hend Syruet and Castain. Pity. He hoped Judge Palmer

would not be too disappointed. Captain Sharpe looked astern as his vessel moved down the bay towards the ocean, and thought to himself that he might well be looking at one of the most beautiful places in the world. Norumbega.

31

This seems an appropriate time to schedule a clambake, which was held over across on the island

There were Mavryck and his ketch boys, Captain Syruet
with crew, Dom Affonso Manuel Etcetera and crew,
the Kincaids, Saint-Castain and Wenamouet, Bernard
Anselme, and Cap'n 'Lon and Elzada. Figured out to
twenty-six, with Barbe, and they held the clambake over
on the sandy beach of Long Razor Island. Norman and
the boys went in a skiff to haul lobster traps, and at low
tide 'Lon and Mavryck dug clams. Elzada, Barbe, and
Nora packed both essentials and frivolities in baskets.
Manny came with a couple of his crew to carry things
down to the wharf. Captain Syruet, asking if he could
help, was told to send men to the island to scrounge for

firewood and lay out the rocks. And as soon as the circle of rocks was ready, Saint-Castain, Bernard Anselme, and Wenamouet took charge of the bake and built a fire. By the time Norman and the boys were back the fire was a roaring hell and Wenamouet favored the gathering with the annual thanksgiving dance of his people—a springtime ritual after the ice gives way and clams can be dug again after a hungry winter. Cap'n 'Lon watched as Wenamouet bent and jumped and writhed and hopped and threw his arms in the air, and after a time opined that the Indians couldn't have been all that hungry or they'd have danced less and eaten sooner. Elzada told Saint-Castain what 'Lon had said, he transferred that to Wenamouet, and Wenamouet reasonably explained that the dance was intended to amuse the people while the fire burned to embers, the stones got hot, and the food was cooked. Elzada, and some of the others, noticed how Barbe was entranced by Wenamouet's dance and responsively jerked her shoulders and wiggled in time to his rhythm. Elzada poked 'Lon to make him notice, and after he watched Barbe a minute he nodded. Then Elzada wanted to know what he was nodding about.

Captain Syruet, now realizing that he had been done a tremendous favor by being intercepted on his way to The Bagaduce, had brought three great bottles of brandy, which more than sufficed, and after the feast there was nothing to do but sit in stuffed lethargy, look off across the water at Morning River, the buildings and cascades, the hills beyond, and to contemplate the excellence of French brandy. Then it startled Elzada, now, to see that Barbe was paying no attention to Wenamouet, whose brandy was being carefully rationed by Saint-Castain, but was hovering over Manny the Portygee, who was feeling no pain. Odd, because Manny had no French and Wenamouet did. But then, Father Hermadore had said Manny communicated, and Elzada could see he was doing all right. "Got to give Barbe some more don'ts," she thought.

Jean Vincent de Saint-Castain, savoring the brandy gently, was telling how he and his Tarratines had watched from the woods as the English ship came to Pentagoët looking for the barrels of wine. Elzada and Mavryck took turns translating, and now and then Mavryck would insert something to round out the story. Castain said that Captain Sharpe had wasted no time in breaking out a derrick and loading the barrels aboard, and it didn't take him long to search the place. Captain Syruet, who didn't need translations, wanted to know how Mavryck had figured out it was his cargo of wines that Sharpe was after.

"Made sense. When we found it wasn't Manny's port they were after, it had to be you. We knew you'd cleared France, and all at once you were at Portsmouth. Why Portsmouth? Been a long time since any French wines came to Portsmouth. Then again, how did it happen Captain Sharpe and his warship were at Pemaquid just when Temple brings charges against Castain? Not hard to figure that out."

"I didn't know about the warship," said Syruet.

"Doesn't seem to me," said Elzada, "that for a man named Sharpe he was all that brainy."

Mavryck executed one of his earth-shaking smiles, and afterwards helped his jaw back in place with one hand. "Remember that he didn't suspect anything."

"But he took those barrels, no questions asked . . ."

"Why not? He was told to go and get a hundred and

two barrels. He found a hundred and two barrels, so he took them. If we'd set out a hundred barrels, he'd have smelt a rat."

"Empty barrels?"

"Now, wait just a damn minute," said Cap'n 'Lon. "That didn't bother me any—I just figured the empty barrels had been filled up."

"That's right."

"Salt water?" asked 'Lon.

"Salt water. Handy and plentiful."

That seemed to bring everything together. Perrot and Temple were not going to relish the way their little surprise had worked out. From the little beach with its clambake, the *Jeannie*, sometimes known as *La Jeanne*, could be seen riding low in the water with her burden of one hundred and two casks of Gironde wine. And there was something comical in the thought of Captain Thomas Sharpe out to the west'ard, homeward bound with one hundred and two casks of salt water from The Bagaduce.

Mavryck stated the matter: "Like to see the face on that damned Judge Palmer when he broaches a hogshead to pledge the health of Governor Temple!"

Cap'n 'Lon said he'd been thinking about filling those casks. "That's one hell of a job," he said, "to bail and pour a hundred and two barrels of salt water. And, the way I break things down—there wasn't all that much time."

Jean Vincent de Saint-Castain listened to Elzada's translation, laughed, and said, "True. Not much time. But the Tarratine nation has many good men, and Wenamouet knew where to find them." He touched his mug of brandy to his lips, and then lowered it so he could add, "It didn't take long."

Cap'n 'Lon said, "But it's still one hell of a big job!"

Jean Vincent de Saint-Castain said, "But tell your husband he forgets—the Tarratine nation also has very good buckets. Ten very good buckets."

32

Now Cap'n 'Lon asks for an accounting about his buckets and barrels, concerning the wines of Pentagoët

Captain Syruet and his *Jeanne* sailed the next morning with one hundred and one barrels of Gironde wines to be set off on the wharf at The Bagaduce. To account for the odd barrel: Captain Syruet worked his *Jeanne* up the Morning River estuary in a masterful manner that Cap'n Alonzo Plaice and Dom Affonso Manuel Henriques Alferes Mor do Póvoa Varzim entre Minho e Doura, as two old coasters should, admired dutifully. For a Frenchman, if the old pirate was a Frenchman, he did all right. Norman had a derrick ready, and the single cask of wine was twitched quickly to the wharf so the *Jeanne* didn't need a makefast. So, with one hundred and one barrels of Gironde wines, Captain Syruet was ready to sail to The Bagaduce. Jean Vincent de Saint-Castain, his son Bernard Anselme, and Wenamouet stepped aboard for a ride home, and the *Jeanne* drifted down the estuary on her way.

Mavryck, watching her go, said, "I doubt like the devil if anybody is going to fool around again with that poor joker Castain. There's nothing I can do about that bahstid down east, but I promise you the wines of Pentagoët are going to be a legend to the west'ard."

'Lon said, "Bet you a cookie Temple and Palmer don't go around telling people."

"They won't have to. I've got four good boys aboard the ketch, and on the way back to Boston we'll talk things over. I been thinking about handing them a little bonus money—thought they might like to buy drinks for some of their friends along the waterfront. Castain is an all-right man, and I'm glad we got enough twos and twos together to save him. They were out to ruin him, for sure."

When Mavryck told Elzada about his idea of spreading gossip through the saloons of Boston and Salem, she said, "Can't think of a better way to spend money. You know, I feel ungodly sorry for that man."

"That man? Castain?"

"Yes. He's sad."

"I didn't see it."

"Maybe you didn't know where to look. He's French, and never wanted to come to Canada. Kicked out of the army, given a piece of land, stuck with the Indians? He's unhappy. Living with a squaw—more than one, I gather. Apple of his eye, darling little Bernard—half savage, never can be a Frenchman. Then, on top of all

that, living halfway French and halfway English he gets
set up by both of them. Only good thing that's happened to him is you—if you hadn't figured that one out
he'd be a goner. He knows that. I talked to him while
you men were taking off the barrel, and I'm right. He
opened with me. If you ever need to count on a friend,
you go hunt up Castain."

"All to the good," said Mavryck. "But I can't say I
was looking for friendship. When I found it wasn't us
they were after, but Castain, I just thought it was a
rotten thing to do anyway—us or him. Besides, I like
to work out puzzles. Anyway, Castain *is* French, he *was*
kicked out of the army, he *does* live with Indians, and
he owns The Bagaduce. Put everything together, and
we'd be fools to let anything happen to Castain. Same
time, he needs us. He trusts us."

"He did, all along. He sent the boy here because he
trusted us."

"Not just the same. He sent the boy here because he
didn't have anybody else to trust. Now he knows he
doesn't need anybody else."

Cap'n 'Lon interrupted. "I was thinking, back there
when you two were buying drinks for Boston drunks,
that we've got some bookkeeping to straighten out. About
my barrels and buckets."

"You've been paid. Paid two-three times over. Just
yell at Elzada—she's had the money credited from
Townes."

"That's no good."

"I thought it was. I was more than generous."

"Sure! Generosity all over the place. Norman got out
the lumber. Out of Elzada's woods. He milled and I
helped. I made the barrels. I made the buckets. The
barrels wind up as a gift to some judge, and the Indians

get free buckets. And you pay Elzada and I have to make more buckets for her to keep her money in. Crazy."

Mavryck looked as if he might be contemplating a smile, but perhaps he thought, considering everything, it would take too much effort. Cap'n 'Lon added, "You know, a fellow likes to see a little money coming in."

Elzada said, " 'Lon's right. I think you better reconsider." Now, Mavryck smiled.

"I do have better things to do. I've got to get back to Boston and find a vessel to pick up some fine *English* wines at The Bagaduce. And find something to deliver there. No profit in sailing an empty boat around. That's it! I just happened to think! I'll bet I know where to get a bargain on a hundred and one empty barrels. Maybe I can get them before they empty them!"

Cap'n 'Lon said, "If you can get a good buy on them, you better pick them up. My barrels are the finest kind."

33

Saint-Castain expresses his thoughts, and Mavryck
writes from Boston to round out the story about the
Gironde wines

Wenamouet brought the letter from Saint-Castain. He
stepped from the woods at mid-morning, came directly
to the kitchen door and tapped. Elzada was alone in the
kitchen and opened to bid him enter, but he shook his
head. He passed her the letter and returned at once into
the woods. She called au revoir to him, but he didn't
answer. Elzada took the letter to the table, sat down,
unfolded it, and began to read. Curious, she thought,
that in all her life she had seen very little handwritten
French. The letter to Jules from Grandfontaine, the letter from Father Hermadore, and a few notes on birch

bark in her girlhood from Marie-Paule—reminders to do this and that. This one was a considerable letter, tediously penned on heavy paper. It was addressed formally to her and 'Lon, but the context showed that Saint-Castain was writing with her, alone, in mind. He knew she would be the one to read the letter.

Castain began with his gratitude for his kind reception at Morning River Farm, for the way his wife had been received, and for the care given his son in a time of anxiety. The tone of the letter was heavy—it was in scholarly French, the kind for formal documents, meant for serious matters. Castain could never, he wrote, begin to express his thanks for the aid in the affair of the wines. He did not understand too well the association of M. Mavryck and Morning River Farm, but would his thanks be extended in turn to M. Mavryck? Elzada smiled at that, because at times she wasn't too sure, either, about that association. Then the formality seemed to fade from Castain's words, and she felt a warmth to what he was writing:

> My mission from both my king and my governor at Quebec is to establish French authority at Pentagoët to the exclusion of the English enemy and to further the prosperity of Acadia and France. Perhaps you will appreciate my consternation when I suddenly found I had enemies among the French and friends among my enemies. I beg you to believe that the experience of your friendship and hospitality has deeply affected me and greatly changed my thinking. As I write, I am in memory with you at the feast by the seaside, amongst a company of people so diverse as to be improbable. Yourselves and your friends, the incredible Portuguese noble-

man, the preposterous Captain Syruet with his pirates, and the formidable M. Mavryck who knows so many things he could not possibly know, along with an incongruous and incomparably beautiful *nègresse* of the strange *patois*. Together with ourselves—an expatriate Frenchman, his son *métis*, and a savage. All in friendship when we might all have been otherwise disposed. A company curiously brought together by the intrigue of the wines of Pentagoët. It was meant, I believe, that we should consider this important, and I do. I do not forget.

Then the tone of the letter shifted again, as if Castain had completed what he truly wanted to say, and he turned again to more formal phrases to end his message. Elzada read the letter through again so she would have the right words in mind when it came to translating it for 'Lon.

When 'Lon came in, he had a letter, too. Manny had been dismantling the remains of one of his old fish houses over an Outer Razor with the idea of taking it to Portugal. 'Lon and Norman had been helping, and board by board and treenail by treenail they had the lumber ready to be put aboard ship. On the way back, they visited the packetbutt. Mavryck wrote in riddle words, so you had to know about barrels of salt water at The Bagaduce to understand. He said certain interests at Boston were embarrassed by the poor quality of wines recently offered, which meant better quality would certainly turn a profit. He was pleased to report that an old friend of his, Captain Philip Syruet of the *Jeanne*, had arrived just yesterday in good health. He was stopping over a few days before returning to France for cargo. He would carry to France on this voyage one hundred and one casks of corned hake. It doesn't pay to sail a boat around with nothing in the hold. Captain Syruet expected to be at The Bagaduce frequently. He did hope, too, that shipments of port wine might become common, as the first cargo of that commodity had been well received in Boston. It had been his great pleasure, he wrote, to make the acquaintance after so long a time of that gentleman of good name and repute—Dom Affonso Manuel Henriques Mor do Póvoa Varzim entre Minho e Doura. They might, should they see him, tell M. Saint-Castain that certain competition both to east'ard and west'ard appears to be eliminated. In conclusion, the manager of Townes Estate expressed his pleasure that things seemed to be doing very well.

There was nothing original about it, because over the years it had been said many times, but Cap'n 'Lon said it now because it seemed as appropriate as ever: "Hate to have that Mavryck for an enemy!"

34

Barbe has her manumission paper, but since it is in French, neither Cap'n 'Lon nor Dom Affonso can read it

Elzada and Barbe had cut up a hen and were making the vegetables ready for a stew. Cap'n 'Lon came into the kitchen after helping Manny get his fish-house lumber stowed. Manny was planning to sail in the morning, bound for the Magdalens and a conference with Father Hermadore. 'Lon took a stool at the table opposite Elzada and said, "How much is Barbe, here, worth on the hoof?"

Elzada said, "Mavryck told me I've got five pounds tied up in her."

"Want to sell her?"

"You thinking of buying?"

"Manny is. Manny wants to buy Barbe."

"What are you talking about?"

"About selling Barbe. Chance for you to make some money. Manny asked me today."

Elzada looked over at Barbe, who was by the fireplace. Barbe couldn't follow the conversation anyway. Elzada said, "What does Manny want her for?"

Cap'n 'Lon tipped his head to one side, grinned, and put it this way, "Well, seeing as how you asked, I think I can confide that he plans to stick her up in a field and scare the hell out of all the crows in Portugal."

"Yes—good idea. But I don't think my question was all that bad. What does Manny want her for?"

"No, it wasn't—that's a good question. Manny wants to marry her. He never married. He's got property and no sons. But on top of that, he thinks Barbe might be a happy answer to his manly desires—if you'll excuse my poetry."

"But, 'Lon—she's Africa!"

"That's no problem with Manny. He's got eyes. His problem is that she's a slave."

"But my God, 'Lon—that's no problem. Manny's welcome to her! But what about Barbe? That's a hell of a way to come by a wife. Give you so much cash, rest next summer in turnips, and do the boots go with her? No—I'm not about to make any deal like that. I can't just up and tell Barbe I sold her off as a wife! I wouldn't, anyway."

'Lon raised a hand. "Maybe I can state the case so it makes more sense. First off, I think Barbe knows something about this already. The way Manny put it, it won't surprise her all that much."

"Wouldn't wonder—Father Hermadore said Manny had a flair for making himself understood."

"Manny does. And he isn't expecting you to hold out for a long price. Same time, he's all heifered up and breathing down his own neck, and not about to quibble over the odd penny. Another thing—Manny noticed the young Indian had an eye for Barbe, and tells me that's all off. He wouldn't know that unless Barbe let him know. Two and two."

"But, 'Lon—she's still Africa. And Indian."

"Want to know something? Manny's own mother was Africa and Turk. He says in Portugal, no matter. The hitch comes on her being a slave. No Portygee gentleman marries a slave. So in a way, he doesn't want to buy her. It's more like a ransom—he'll pay, and you set her free. Then he'll up-sail for Father Hermadore, who—they tell me—knows how to bring off a real good wedding. He'll jingle his bell and make her a ladyship. And even Father Hermadore, Manny says, wouldn't touch the thing with a fourteen-foot oar if she was still a slave."

Elzada called, "Barbe—viens 'ci!" and as Barbe came over from the fireplace Elzada said to 'Lon, "Maybe we've got the answer of what to do with Barbe." She took Barbe's hands in hers and spoke to her softly for a few minutes, and 'Lon could see that Barbe had not been taken by surprise. "Son of a sea cook!" he thought.

"So the next question," Elzada resumed with 'Lon, "is how to go about taking off the shackles. What did God do when everybody came out of Egypt? Do I hold up my hand and spit in the wind? Must be some kind of legal stuff."

"Take five pounds from Manny and give him a bill of sale. Then give him the five pounds as a wedding present. I don't think anybody'll ever come back on that. I can give you the words for a bill of sale—'Know all men by these presents . . .' "

"Bill of sale is no good. She needs something different. Mavryck said I could sign a paper, but he didn't tell me what to write on it."

"All right," said 'Lon. "Here's what you do. You give Barbe something that says you set her free, and set down a promise to give her something better later. Then have Mavryck put the lawyers to it and make a record in Boston. No problem!"

Elzada said to Barbe, "Pas de problème!"

When Manny came up from his schooner, his proposal to Barbe was through Elzada. Elzada told Barbe that Manny wanted to marry her, and Barbe said she knew that. Elzada remembered how Barbe was uneasy about joining the others at table when she first came to Morning River Farm. Slaves didn't do that. But tonight, Barbe was family, and sat beside Manny for a chicken-stew reception. She was radiant. She was beautiful. And she was free. She showed Manny the paper that said she was free, but Manny shook his head.

Cap'n 'Lon said, "Don't feel bad—it's French, and I can't read it either."

Elzada had a half-dozen books to go to Father Hermadore, along with a good letter to the rascal priest about Barbe. Manny and Barbe stood on the after deck of the schooner as a light morning air gave a flutter to the rising sails. The schooner eased into motion. Norman came from the boat shop with his musket and fired a godspeed salute.

Manny and Barbe were waving. A sailor at the taffrail answered Norman with a pistol shot. It took maybe half a minute after the puff of smoke before the sound rode up the estuary so 'Lon, and Elzada, and the Kincaids, heard it.

Cap'n 'Lon said, "Poor old Manny!"

CREDITS, SOURCES, AND ACKNOWLEDGMENTS

Le Baron de Saint-Castin, Pierre Daviault (Montreal, 1939)
The Land of St. Castine, Herbert Milton Sylvester (Boston, 1909)
History of France, Henri Martin, Vol. 1 (Boston, 1865)
Maine Historical Society Collections, Vol. 7, John E. Godfrey, *The Baron de Saint Castin* (1876)
The Noble Grapes and Great Wines of France, André L. Simon
Tales of a Wayside Inn, the student's second tale, Henry Wadsworth Longfellow
History of Maine, John S. C. Abbott
Gazetteer of the State of Maine, George J. Varney, Boston
Castine Quadrangle, U.S.G.S.
Webster's Geographical Dictionary
Arthur Monke, Bowdoin College Library
Howard B. Gotlieb, Judith Podolsky, Charles Niles, Boston University Libraries
Papers of Governor Andros
Shirley Grunert Martin, Mantor Library, University of Maine at Farmington
Dr. Olin Sewall Pettingill, Wayne, Maine
M. Henry Delorme, North Hatley, Quebec
Dorothy Bellhouse, Friendship, Maine
Le Saint-Laurent et ses Iles, Damase Potvin (Quebec, 1945)
Cynthia English, Library of the Boston Athenaeum

The Voyages of Jacques Cartier, Public Archives of Canada, 1924

Philip F. Purrington, Old Dartmouth Historical Society Whaling Museum, New Bedford

Jesuit Relations

Maine My State, Maine Writers Research Club (Lewiston, Maine, 1919)

Nouveaux Voyages, La Hontan

Mr. and Mrs. Raymond Cote, Biddeford, Maine

Garneau's History of Canada

Sullivan, *History of Maine*

Massachusetts Historical Collections, French Archives

History of the Negro Race in America, 1619 to 1880, Putnam's (New York, 1885)

Sketch of the Laws Relating to Slavery, Stroud (Negro Universities Press, New York, 1856)

The Law of Freedom and Bondage in the United States, Hurd (Negro Universities Press, New York, 1968) (originally published in 1858 by Little, Brown)

The Slave Power, Cairnes (Macmillan, London, 1863)

Johns Hopkins University Studies, *The Free Negro in America*, Russell

Paul Wolter, Camden, Maine

Captain Alan Bellhouse, Friendship, Maine

Karyn Christy, Sebago Lake, Maine

Julia Christy, Sebago Lake, Maine

St. Augustine, *Epistle to Januarius*

Witherle Memorial Library, Castine, Maine

Francis W. Hatch, late of Castine

Dorothea Cox, Cape North, Nova Scotia

History of the Abenaquis, Abbot Maurault

Wild Flowers, F. W. Stack (New York, 1909)

Readings in English History, E. P. Cheyney, 1922

Lucia S. Goodwin, *Monticello*, Charlottesville, Virginia

Floyd Cormack, Jean Palmer, Millicent Pendleton, Emerson
 Bullard
Francine Pichette, Montreal Public Libraries
Eleanor MacLean, Librarian, Blacker-Wood Library of Zool-
 ogy and Ornithology, McGill University, Montreal